THE WICKED WIT OF
WILLIAM
SHAKESPEARE

427 Quotes, Excerpts, and Passages

Edited by
DOMINIQUE ENRIGHT

GRAMERCY BOOKS
NEW YORK

This 2007 edition is published by Gramercy Books, an imprint of Random House Value Publishing, a division of Random House, Inc., New York, by agreement with Michael O'Mara Books Limited.

Gramercy Books is a registered trademark and the colophon is a trademark of Random House, Inc.

Random House
New York • Toronto • London • Sydney • Auckland
www.valuebooks.com

A catalog record for this title is available from the Library of Congress.

ISBN: 978-0-517-22937-8

Printed and bound in the United States of America.

10 9 8 7 6 5 4 3 2 1

Contents

Introduction:

Shakespeare the Man

SHAKESPEARE is recognized worldwide as the soul of English literature, and as one of the few truly great dramatists of all time, yet his life was unremarkable – indeed, his gift as poet and dramatist aside, the most remarkable thing about his life is that he did live: he was born during an epidemic of the plague, which wiped out a substantial proportion of Stratford's population, including near neighbours of the Shakespeares.

An entry in the baptism records of Stratford-upon-Avon's Holy Trinity Church reads: '1564 April 26 Gulielmus filius Johannes Shakspere', and as it was traditional to baptize a child about three days after birth, 23 April – St George's Day – has been settled on as Shakespeare's birthday. His father was John Shakespeare, a glover and leather-worker; Mary, his mother, was the youngest of eight daughters of a well-to-do farmer called Robert Arden (whose family had given its name to the Forest of Arden), who had died the year before she married John Shakespeare (it is thought in 1557) when she was eighteen. For John Shakespeare, already beginning to make his way up the local social hierarchy, marriage to a girl of 'good family' was a good step up in the world. By 1561 he was a burgess, a town councillor, and then a chamberlain, in charge of the borough's financial affairs; in 1565 he was elected an alderman and in 1568 Bailiff of Stratford. In 1575, when William was eleven, he applied for a coat of arms. But perhaps his meteoric rise had tempted him to overreach himself, for at this point his fortunes took a downturn, and it was not until 1596 that he followed up his application for a coat of arms and was granted it (the motto was Non Sanz

Droict – 'not without right' – but does not seem ever to have been used).

The Shakespeares' first child, Joan, was born in 1558 and died in infancy; Margaret was born in 1562 but died the following year. William was born in 1564; he was followed by Gilbert (1566), another Joan (1569), Anne (1571), who died aged only eight, Richard (1574), and Edmund (1580). As the sons of a prominent citizen, William and his brothers would have received a sound education at a good grammar school. Children were worked hard at school – from early morning until about five, with a two-hour break for lunch and maybe two or three short breaks. Pupils were required to write and speak in Latin – then a lingua franca among statesmen and scholars – and were given training in classical literature, rhetoric, and oratory. Ben Jonson's famous remark that Shakespeare had 'small Latin and less Greek' should not be taken literally and certainly not judged by today's standards. Jonson himself was extremely learned, and his knowledge of the classics would today be awe-inspiring: Shakespeare could not compete – but today his mastery of the classics, if inferior to that of Jonson, would be regarded as considerable.

By the time young William left school, at the age of fourteen or fifteen, his parents would have been struggling with debts, while trying to cope with a small boy. Soon there was to be the death of a little girl to add to their miseries, and then a new baby. William must have had to start earning a living straight away. No records have been found to tell us exactly what he did, though traditionally an eldest son would join his father's business as an apprentice, with a view to his taking over the concern in due course. John Aubrey in his *Brief Lives* (1681) claims that Stratford locals told him that when Shakespeare was 'a boy he exercised his father's Trade', but as they also claimed that John Shakespeare was a butcher, their information seems less than reliable. John Aubrey was also told, perhaps more reliably, by the son of a theatrical associate of Shakespeare's, Christopher Beeston, that Shakespeare 'had been in his younger yeares a Schoolmaster in the Countrey'. Whatever he did, though, there is no reason to suppose that Shakespeare did not have more than one job during the years between his leaving school and his emergence in London as a playwright and actor in 1592.

In November 1582, at the unusually young age of eighteen, William Shakespeare married twenty-six-year-old Anne Hathaway, the daughter of a prosperous local landowner. Their daughter Susanna was born the following May, and twins, Judith and Hamnet, were born in early 1585. It is almost certain that they lived with William's family until he was doing well enough to buy New Place (the second largest house in Stratford) in 1597. It is, however, possible that Shakespeare himself left Stratford for London as early as 1586 or 1587. Why he did so is not known, though theories abound; one of the most popular stories is that he was caught poaching deer in nearby Charlecote Park, owned by Sir Thomas Lucy, and fled to London to avoid prosecution. Justice Shallow in *The Merry Wives of Windsor* is said to be based on Sir Thomas Lucy.

Alternatively, Shakespeare might simply have long been interested in the stage and was one day made an offer he could not refuse. It is known that in June 1587 one member of the troupe of actors known as the Queen's Men, who were in the area at the time, died in a duel. They would have needed a replacement in a hurry and perhaps William Shakespeare jumped at the chance. For the ensuing years, until about 1611, it has to be assumed that Shakespeare spent most of his time in London, while making reasonably frequent visits home.

Whatever happened, it is clear that by 1592 he was well-known enough as a playwright and actor to be the object of a jealous attack from fellow dramatist, Robert Greene. While it is impossible to date Shakespeare's plays accurately, it is thought that by then he had written some five or six, and the poem *Venus and Adonis*, which was dedicated to Henry Wriothesley, Earl of Southampton, whose patronage he hoped to gain, and did. By 1594 he was a member of the Lord Chamberlain's company of actors – the Chamberlain's Men – by whom he was employed not only as an actor but also as a playwright. In December of that year the company played twice at the palace in Greenwich during the Queen's Christmas festivities: William Kemp, Richard Burbage and William Shakespeare are named in the royal household accounts as having been paid for their performances.

In 1596, Shakespeare's only son, Hamnet, died. His play *King John* is thought to have been written (or revised) around then: 'Grief fills the room up of my absent child,/Lies in his bed, walks up and down with me . . .' (III, iv). Perhaps he was thinking of his dead son; one might also speculate that he tried to overcome his grief by throwing himself into his work with greater intensity than ever. For over the next two to three years, he seems to have written about seven plays and soon established himself as a playwright and poet of note. 'As Plautus and Seneca are accounted the best for comedy and tragedy among the Latins, so Shakespeare among the English is most excellent for both kinds for the stage,' commented the writer Francis Meres, in his commonplace book, *Palladis Tamia: Wits Treasury* (1598). He goes on: 'for Comedy, witnes his Gentlemen of Verona, his Errors, his Love labors lost, his Love labours wonne, his Midsummer night dreame, & his Merchant of Venice: for Tragedy his Richard the 2. Richard the 3. Henry the 4. King John, Titus Andronicus and his Romeo and Juliet.' Scholars have puzzled over '*Love's Labour's Won*', but it is generally supposed to be an alternative title of *The Taming of the Shrew*.

Shakespeare became a shareholder in the Chamberlain's Men – whose members included such eminent theatrical figures as James Burbage and his sons – Cuthbert, manager and businessman, and Richard, the famous tragedian – and the comedian Will Kemp, as well as Shakespeare himself. It is very likely that he had considerable talent as an actor, for his fellow dramatist Ben Jonson lists his name as both one of the principal comedians and one of the principal tragedians in his – Jonson's – own plays. In addition, Shakespeare was in the happy position of producing a steady stream of works of extraordinary quality and variety – tragedies, comedies, poetry – and making a profit from them. He showed himself to be an astute businessman as well, his investment in the Chamberlain's Men proving – probably thanks to the plays (his) that its actors performed – to be a profitable one. His father's return to financial stability, and his coat of arms, were probably owed at least in part to him. In 1597 Shakespeare was able to buy New Place in Stratford, into which he moved his wife and daughters. Over the next few years he acquired more property in Stratford and bought a share of the tax revenues of some agricultural land in Welcombe, near Stratford, all of which suggests he was prospering. The only property in London he bought was the Blackfriars Gatehouse, in early 1613, which he seems to have acquired purely as an investment, as he leased it immediately. He had by then gone back to live full-time in Stratford.

Until 1597 the Chamberlain's Men performed mainly at The Theatre in Shoreditch, London's first public playhouse, built in 1576 by James Burbage. The lease on the land on which it stood expired in April, shortly after Burbage's death, and the landlord, who apparently did not approve of theatrical goings-on, would not renew the lease. So the Burbage brothers proceeded to dismantle The Theatre, much to the landlord's disgust, and build a new theatre in Southwark, which they completed in late 1599. The brothers were able only to pay fifty per cent of the costs so five of the shareholders in the company, including Shakespeare, bought shares in the theatre as well. This was the Globe. It proved a profitable venture (in spite of a cannon burning the theatre down during a performance of *Henry VIII* in 1613; it was rapidly rebuilt – with tiles replacing the thatched roof). In 1608 the Burbages bought back the lease of a theatre built by their father in Blackfriars. Unlike the Globe, the Blackfriars theatre was enclosed, with a roof over the stage as well as the audience, so the King's Men (as the company was now called) used it more during the winter, the Globe during the summer.

The reigns of Elizabeth and that of her successor, James I, were full of political intrigue; plots and conspiracies seemed to abound and, if they did not exist, were invented. It was easy – and sometimes fatal – to fall out of favour. As live entertainment, plays, even more than books, could influence public opinion, and actors and writers often got involved in politics. So the court kept a close eye on them; before a new play could be performed the text had to be submitted to the Lord Chamberlain for approval, and not infrequently had to be cut, rewritten or even dropped entirely. Shakespeare himself, politically conservative and clever enough to disguise any controversial opinions he wished to air, only once came near to falling foul of the censors. This was when, in 1601, the Earl of Essex, having given up his futile attempts to reinstate himself as the Queen's favourite, organized instead a rebellion against her. On the day before the uprising was to take place, the Chamberlain's Men put on a performance especially requested by Essex and his followers – Shakespeare's 'play of the deposing and killing of King Richard II'. Questions were asked, but the court was satisfied that the players were innocent of any involvement in the conspiracy. Indeed, in a matter of weeks they were performing before the court. The Earl of Essex, however, was executed for treason – and, more worrying for Shakespeare,

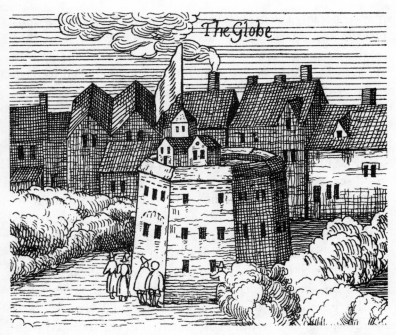

The Globe

his friend and patron, Henry Wriothesley, Earl of Southampton, was also condemned to death. In the event, his sentence was commuted to life imprisonment, and when James I succeeded Elizabeth, he was released, eventually to become a favoured courtier.

When, on the death of Elizabeth I in 1603, James I (James VI of Scotland) came to the throne, he granted royal patronage to the King's Men who thus continued to be court favourites. Indeed, it would seem that no company performed more at court over the next few years. Between the end of 1604 and the end of 1605, the King's Men performed eleven times before the King – and seven of these performances were of plays by Shakespeare: *The Comedy of Errors*, *Love's Labour's Lost*, *The Merry Wives of Windsor*, *Othello*, *Measure for Measure*, and *The Merchant of Venice* (twice). During the early years of this new century, Shakespeare wrote his most outstanding

[13]

plays – notably the great tragedies such as *Hamlet*, *King Lear*, *Othello* and *Macbeth*, and also the late plays that fit into neither of the categories of comedy and tragedy, such as *The Winter's Tale* and *The Tempest*. The latter is believed to have been written in 1611 and to be the last play written solely by Shakespeare.

From 1611 he seems to have spent most of his time in Stratford, having apparently given up acting some years before. 'The latter part of his life was spent, as all men of good sense will wish theirs may be, in ease, retirement, and the conversation of his friends. He had the good fortune to gather an estate equal to his occasion, and, in that, to his wish; and is said to have spent some years before his death at his native Stratford,' wrote his earliest biographer, Nicholas Rowe, in 1709. 'His pleasurable wit, and good nature, engaged him in the acquaintance, and entitled him to the friendship of the gentlemen of the neighbourhood'. He did not, however, abandon writing completely, and collaborated with John Fletcher, his successor as the King's Men's dramatist, in, as far as is known, three plays, none of them of any real distinction – *Henry VIII* (written between 1611 and early 1613, and probably best remembered for being the play that burned down the Globe), *The Two Noble Kinsmen* (probably written in 1613 or the following year) and the now lost *Cardenio*, which was probably also written around 1613.

In 1607, Susanna Shakespeare had married John Hall, a highly thought-of doctor who had settled in Stratford some years earlier and who was to become a friend of Shakespeare's. Her sister Judith was to make a less happy match: in 1616 she married a wine merchant, Thomas Quiney, by whom she was probably pregnant; unfortunately, another woman was also pregnant by him and died in childbirth a month after the wedding. William Shakespeare clearly did not trust his new son-in-law and altered his will so that Quiney would not be able to get his hands on Judith's inheritance. Of his family, Susanna seems to have been his main beneficiary – his wife Anne famously receiving only the 'second-best bed'. This bequest has led to much speculation about the state of his marriage and assertions that it was intended as a snub, but it has been pointed out that the best bed would have been reserved for guests while the second-best was probably the one she had slept in during all of her married life; traditionally, a widow would remain in her own home after the death of her husband, so he would not have to make any special provision in that area; and, as there is no record that Anne Shakespeare lived in poverty after his death, it must be assumed that her daughters would have seen to it that she wanted for nothing (it may be that Shakespeare had discussed the matter with them beforehand). The will was drawn up in January 1616, and Shakespeare rewrote it to protect Judith's inheritance towards the end of March. And on 23 April 1616 – thought to be his fifty-second birthday – he died.

It is not known what he died of. In an age when much of what we take for granted today – from fridges to antibiotics – was non-existent, and standards of hygiene and cleanliness were not of the highest, disease was rife. Epidemics of influenza, bubonic plague and smallpox regularly cut a swathe through the world's populations; in 1617, Shakespeare's son-in-law John Hall recorded a 'new fever', possibly typhus, which struck Stratford in 1616. There is no indication, however, that this was the cause of Shakespeare's death. His comparatively early retirement in 1611 might have been because of failing health; he wrote his will such a short time before his death that it could have been because he knew he had not long to live. And why had he stopped writing, other than the collaborations with Fletcher (which could be seen more as helping Fletcher into his role as Shakespeare's successor as the King's Men's resident playwright)? It could have been because he was too busy with his properties in both Stratford and London, and enjoying, as Nicholas Rowe had surmised, 'ease, retirement, and the conversation of his friends', but it could also have been because he felt, with Prospero (*The Tempest*, IV, i), that 'Our revels now are ended' . . .

> . . . We are such stuff
> As dreams are made on, and our little life
> Is rounded with a sleep.

Shakespeare was one of the most popular playwrights of his day, a successful actor and a shrewd businessman. But what was he like, this man who would one day be recognized worldwide as a literary genius? Indications are that he was well-liked and had many friends. Nicholas Rowe, quoted above, remarks on his 'pleasurable wit and good nature', a posthumous appraisal, but supported by others. In his *Brief Lives* (1681), John Aubrey cites the son of the actor Christopher Beeston, a friend of Shakespeare's, who told him how his father had described William Shakespeare as 'a handsome, well-shaped man – very good company, and of a very ready and pleasant smooth wit'. Also, 'the more to be admired that he was not a company keeper [and] wouldn't be debauched'.

Some forty-odd years after Shakespeare's death, Thomas Fullerton wrote:

> Many were the wit-combats betwixt him and Ben Jonson; which two I behold like a Spanish great galleon and an English man-of-war; Master Jonson (like the former) was built far higher in learning; solid, but slow, in his performances. Shakespeare, with the English man-of-war, lesser in bulk, but lighter in sailing, could turn with all tides, tack about, and take advantage of all winds, by the quickness of his wit and invention.

Of Shakespeare's contemporaries, Ben Jonson's words are the most famous – perhaps because, while he was not stinting of admiration, he was also prepared to criticize him, saying at one point that he wished that Shakespeare had blotted out a thousand lines. But: '. . . I loved the man, and do honour his memory (on this side idolatry) as much as any,' he wrote; 'he was (indeed) honest, and of an open and free nature; had an excellent fancy, brave notions, and gentle expressions; wherein he flowed with that facility that sometimes it was necessary he should be stopped.'

The First Folio of Shakespeare's plays, published in 1623, contains letters and poems by friends and admirers. One, by Ben Jonson, includes the lines:

> Thou art a Monument without a tomb
> And art alive still, while thy Booke doth live,
> And we have wits to read, and praise to give.

The Wicked Wit of William Shakespeare

> 'O wicked wit and gifts, that have the power
> So to seduce!'

Thus railed the ghost of Hamlet's father. He was talking about his brother Claudius, but this exclamation could be applied to Shakespeare, whose wicked wit and gifts are his ability with words – his language has indeed the power to seduce us, today as four hundred years ago. 'He was not of an age, but for all time!' Ben Jonson's words, in his memorial to 'My Beloved, the Author, Mr William Shakespeare', written in 1623, have, unlike many eulogies for dead friends, proved true.

For all the admiration heaped upon Shakespeare before his death and during the centuries after it, there have also been detractors – some unreasonable or at least disgruntled: 'I have tried lately to read Shakespeare, and found it so intolerably dull that it nauseated me,' complained the naturalist Charles Darwin – and some whose criticism has been more balanced: '. . . if much of our praise is paid by perception and judgement, much is likewise given by custom and veneration. We fix our eyes upon his graces and turn them from his deformities, and endure in him what we should in another loathe and despise,' commented Dr Johnson. Ben Jonson himself, as quoted earlier, was far from uncritical (although some of his grumblings smack of nose-out-of-jointness). But the general view is that Shakespeare was arguably the greatest dramatist ever, and the greatest figure in English literature, for which reason, as Johnson observes, his faults are overlooked. This is perhaps because he strikes a chord within us, perhaps because his audience and readers respond to his sympathetic understanding of human frailties; his concern with right and wrong, good and evil, and how they seem to overlap, so that a potentially 'good' person may commit an evil act; a 'bad' character may show kindness (Claudius and Gertrude are kind to Ophelia). At the same time, while celebrating the dignity of human emotions, he is able to demonstrate 'what fools these mortals be' (as Puck in *A Midsummer Night's Dream* remarks) – through the stupid things they say or do, or the astute points made by the clowns, fools or sprites. There is, too, a strong vein of pragmatism and common sense, not only in his plays but also in his poems – if snow is white, well, then my mistress's breast are dun, he says in one of the wonderful sonnets, an ironic outlook that pervades the plays too.

The English essayist (and original bluestocking), Elizabeth Montagu wrote in 1769: 'Shakespeare seemed to have had the art of the Dervish in the Arabian tales who could throw his soul

into the body of another man and be at once possessed of his sentiments, adopt his passions and rise to all the functions and feelings of his situation.' (*An Essay on the Writing and Genius of Shakespeare Compared with Greek and French Dramatic Poets.*) This actor's ability to get under the skin of any character must surely account in large part for his universal popularity. That, and his extraordinary gift with words – not just the beauty of his language, but the way his words go straight to the heart: the passion and wisdom, the compassion, sympathy, and a profound understanding of human behaviour in those words – and also a simple enjoyment of words: there are jokes and puns (often of the kind that today elicit a mock groan) throughout Shakespeare's writing. However, while the comic characters relish word play, moments of intense passion or despair also give rise to verbal acrobatics: words are twisted to follow down dark paths, puns are savage – 'O that this too, too sullied/solid flesh would melt . . .' (Hamlet, filled with grief and disgust by his father's sudden death and his mother's marriage to his uncle, now king; worse is to come). So many of his phrases have become a part of the language that we do not even realize they originated with – or were popularized by – Shakespeare. We quote him every day, knowingly and unknowingly, and, like the Bible, his works have provided countless book titles. The characters in his plays are larger than life, their energies superhuman, their passions frightening in their intensity; they are real but not realistic; the plots quite often unremarkable – and, sometimes, most unrealistic; the histories not to be taken as history. But they all – plots and characters – serve as a vehicle for a profound comment on the human condition.

The wicked wit? In the sense of humour and mischief, most of this is to be found in Shakespeare's dialogues – often, not always, between a 'clown' or 'fool' and a 'straight' character. Some of these are reproduced here – but apart from the fact that they can be lengthy, many of them need to be in context to make sense and to amuse (neither do they always fit in any category). Many of the quotations in this collection cannot be described as 'comic', 'humorous' or 'playful', but (before accusations of contravening the Trades Description Act start pouring in) one of the meanings of 'wit' is 'awareness or cognizance' – or 'wisdom'; to be witty is not just to be brilliantly amusing, but can mean to be intelligent, clever or skilful – and this would apply to Shakespeare's use of language. The word 'wicked' (setting aside its current slang meanings of 'very good', 'brilliant', 'clever', which must all surely apply to Shakespeare's writing) can mean mischievous or sly; it can be twisted to mean manipulative – as in the quotation opening this chapter – manipulative and seductive, beguiling our senses, rousing our emotions. Why else should we be so moved by the words we read or hear on stage, feel such sympathy for that passionate but indecisive young man, compassion for murderers, pity for a self-important fool, admiration for a flawed being?

No More Cakes and Ale: Drink and Food

FOOD AND DRINK are down to earth and, on stage, serve to alter the mood, to bring the action down from dramatic heights, or, in a comedy, to underline the humour. Drink especially has plenty to offer: there is one scene in *Macbeth* to provide the audience with comic relief – and it owes its humour to the less-than-sober porter and his views on drink. Sir Toby Belch and Falstaff are splendid figures of fun largely because they are much given to eating and drinking – for which, however, they may be mocked. Descriptions of swinishly inebriated men snoring in soiled beds or committing outrages when dangerously under the influence, on the other hand, serve to turn the audience against them. And, of course, making someone insensibly drunk is a good way of getting them out of the way . . .

Saint George, that swinged the dragon, and e'er since
Sits on his horse back at mine hostess' door.
                    PHILIP THE BASTARD, alluding to inn signs,
                                        King John, II, i

PORTER: . . . and drink, sir, is a great provoker of three
    things.
MACDUFF: What three things does drink especially provoke?
PORTER: Marry, sir, nose-painting, sleep, and urine. Lechery,
    sir, it provokes, and unprovokes; it provokes the desire, but
    it takes away the performance.
                                        Macbeth, II, iii

Drunkenness is his best virtue, for he will be swine-drunk;
and in his sleep he does little harm, save to his bed-
clothes about him.
                    PAROLLES, of the non-existent 'Captain Dumain',
                                All's Well That Ends Well, IV, iii

His two chamberlains
Will I with wine and wassail so convince
That memory, the warder of the brain,
Shall be a fume, and the receipt of reason
A limbeck only: when in swinish sleep
Their drenched natures lie as in a death.
                    LADY MACBETH, *Macbeth*, I, vii

I have very poor and unhappy brains for drinking: I could well wish courtesy would invent some other custom of entertainment.

Cassio's confession is ill-advised: Iago exploits his weakness and Cassio is persuaded to drink more:

Do not think, gentlemen, I am drunk: this is my ancient; this is my right hand, and this is my left: I am not drunk now; I can stand well enough, and speak well enough.
ALL: Excellent well.
CASSIO: Why, very well then; you must not think then that I am drunk.

The result is that Cassio gets involved in a fight, and is shamed before Othello, who regretfully dismisses him. Cassio is disgusted with himself:

Drunk? and speak parrot? and squabble? swagger? swear? and discourse fustian with one's own shadow? O thou invisible spirit of wine, if thou hast no name to be known by, let us call thee devil! . . . O God, that men should put an enemy in their mouths to steal away their brains! that we should, with joy, pleasance revel and applause, transform ourselves into beasts!

CASSIO, Othello, II, iii

Come, come, good wine is a good familiar creature, if it be well used: exclaim no more against it.

IAGO, Othello, II, iii

You come in faint for want of meat, depart reeling with too much drink; sorry that you have paid too much, and sorry that you are paid too much; purse and brain both empty; the brain the heavier for being too light, the purse too light, being drawn of heaviness.

FIRST GAOLER, *Cymbeline*, V, iv

I would give all my fame for a pot of ale, and safety.

BOY, *King Henry V*, III, ii

A' never broke any man's head but his own, and that was against a post when he was drunk.

BOY, of Nym, *King Henry V*, III, ii

TOBY BELCH: 'Tis a gentleman here – a plague o' these pickle-herring!

Sir Toby Belch is living up to his name. It is not pickled herrings that are to blame – or the only things that are pickled – as Olivia sees quite clearly . . .

OLIVIA: What's a drunken man like, fool?

CLOWN (FESTE): Like a drowned man, a fool and a mad man: one draught above heat makes him a fool; the second mads him; and a third drowns him.

OLIVIA: Go thou and seek the crowner, and let him sit o' my coz; for he's in the third degree of drink, he's drowned: go, look after him.

Twelfth Night, I, v

[24]

A good sherris sack hath a two-fold operation in it. It ascends me into the brain; dries me there all the foolish and dull and curdy vapours which environ it; makes it apprehensive, quick, forgetive, full of nimble fiery and delectable shapes, which, delivered o'er to the voice, the tongue, which is the birth, becomes excellent wit. The second property of your excellent sherris is, the warming of the blood; which, before cold and settled, left the liver white and pale, which is the badge of pusillanimity and cowardice; but the sherris warms it and makes it course from the inwards to the parts extreme: it illumineth the face, which as a beacon gives warning to all the rest of this little kingdom, man, to arm; and then the vital commoners and inland petty spirits muster me all to their captain, the heart, who, great and puffed up with this retinue, doth any deed of courage; and this valour comes of sherris.

FALSTAFF, waxing lyrical about drink,
King Henry IV, Part 2, IV, iii

Dost thou think, because thou art virtuous, there shall be no more cakes and ale?

SIR TOBY BELCH, *Twelfth Night*, II, iii

But to my mind, though I am native here
And to the manner born, it is a custom
More honour'd in the breach than the observance.

HAMLET, referring to draining a goblet of wine

in one gulp, *Hamlet*, I, iv

Why, sir, for my part I say the gentleman had drunk
himself out of his five sentences.

BARDOLPH, *The Merry Wives of Windsor*, I, i

Sir Hugh Evans is quick to correct him: 'It is his five senses: fie,
what the ignorance is!'

He's a sworn rioter: he has a sin that often
Drowns him, and takes his valour prisoner:
If there were no foes, that were enough
To overcome him: in that beastly fury
He has been known to commit outrages,
And cherish factions: 'tis inferr'd to us,
His days are foul and his drink dangerous.

SECOND SENATOR, *Timon of Athens*, III, v

They were red-hot with drinking;
So full of valour that they smote the air
For breathing in their faces; beat the ground
For kissing of their feet.

ARIEL, *The Tempest*, IV, i

DOMITIUS ENOBARBUS: Ay, sir; we did sleep day out of
countenance, and made the night light with drinking.
MECÆNAS: Eight wild-boars roasted whole at a breakfast,
and but twelve persons there; is this true?
ENOBARBUS: This was but as a fly by an eagle: we had much
more monstrous matter of feast, which worthily deserved
noting.

Antony and Cleopatra, II, ii

Truly, a peck of provender: I could munch your good dry
oats. Methinks I have a great desire to a bottle of hay:
good hay, sweet hay, hath no fellow.

BOTTOM, in his ass's head,
A Midsummer Night's Dream, IV, i

*'Bottle' is a slip of the tongue – 'bundle' is what he meant, but
perhaps his thoughts were with a bottle of ale.*

'Tis an ill cook that cannot lick his own fingers.

SECOND SERVANT TO CAPULET,
outlining his plan for choosing cooks,
Romeo and Juliet, IV, ii

[27]

Captain Fluellen is forcing Pistol – who does not like leeks – to eat one, raw.

I peseech you heartily, scurvy, lousy knave, at my desires, and my requests, and my petitions, to eat, look you, this leek: because, look you, you do not love it, nor your affections and your appetites and your disgestions doo's not agree with it, I would desire you to eat it . . . if you can mock a leek, you can eat a leek.

PISTOL: By this leek, I will most horribly revenge: I eat and eat, I swear.

King Henry V, V, i

I am a great eater of beef and I believe that does harm to my wit.

SIR ANDREW AGUECHEEK, *Twelfth Night,* I, iii

He hath eaten me out of house and home; he hath put all my substance into that fat belly of his.

MISTRESS QUICKLY, of Falstaff,
King Henry IV, Part 2, II, i

Here's that which is too weak to be a sinner, honest water, which ne'er left man i' the mire.

APEMANTUS, *Timon of Athens,* I, ii

These words are engraved on the water fountain in Stratford's market square.

Things sweet to taste prove in digestion sour.
JOHN OF GAUNT, *King Richard II*, I, iii

Leave gormandizing; know the grave doth gape
For thee thrice wider than for other men.
HENRY IV, to Falstaff, *King Henry IV, Part 2*, V, v

Unquiet meals make ill digestions.
AMELIA, *The Comedy of Errors*, V, i

I must have saffron to colour the warden pies; mace;
dates? – none, that's out of my note; nutmegs, seven; a
race or two of ginger, but that I may beg; four pound of
prunes, and as many of raisins o' the sun.
CLOWN (the Shepherd's son), planning the
sheep-shearing feast, *The Winter's Tale*, IV, iii

Desperate Mart: the Professions

I N PLAYS, as – often – in life, a character's job helps to give the audience an idea of his or her place in the scheme of things. In Shakespeare's dramas the audience knows that the king, whether good or bad, is powerful, but that his life is at risk if he doesn't keep up repayments; that a peasant or labourer is probably a comic character, unless he's a ruffian; that a doctor is a minor character, well-meaning but not always effective; that a usurer is greedy, a politician ambitious . . .

Thou art not for the fashion of these times,
Where none will sweat but for promotion.
                    ORLANDO, to his loyal servant, Adam,
                              As You Like It, II, iii

I had thought to have let in some of all professions that go
the primrose way to the everlasting bonfire.

PORTER, Macbeth, I, iii

*Less than sober, and unnerved by loud knocking, the Porter
imagines himself porter at the gates of hell: in his fantasizing he
has admitted a greedy farmer, an 'equivocator' and a thieving
tailor, but now he decides it's too cold for hell, and goes to answer
the knocking at the gate.*

There is boundless theft
In limited professions.

TIMON, to baffled bandits,
Timon of Athens, IV, iii

*He has congratulated the bandits on at least admitting to being
thieves, bitterly claiming that professions such as medicine and
the law are full of thieves.*

'Tis a common proof,
That lowliness is young ambition's ladder,
Whereto the climber-upward turns his face;
But when he once attains the upmost round,
He then unto the ladder turns his back,
Looks in the clouds, scorning the base degrees
By which he did ascend.

BRUTUS, Julius Caesar, II, i

How like a fawning publican he looks!

SHYLOCK, of Antonio,
The Merchant of Venice, I, iii

My nature is subdued
To what it works in, like the dyer's hand.

SONNET CXI

Let me have no lying; it becomes none but tradesmen.

AUTOLYCUS, *The Winter's Tale*, IV, iii

And Autolycus knows all about lying . . .

Let us, like merchants, show our foulest wares,
And think, perchance, they'll sell; if not,
The lustre of the better yet to show,
Shall show the better.

ULYSSES, to Nestor, *Troilus and Cressida*, I, iii

Sir, I am a true labourer: I earn that I eat, get that I wear,
owe no man hate, envy no man's happiness, glad of other
men's good, content with my harm, and the greatest of my
pride is to see my ewes graze and my lambs suck.

CORIN, to Touchstone, *As You Like It*, III, ii

Our tradesmen within their shops and going
About their functions friendly.
SICINIUS, to Brutus, *Coriolanus*, IV, vi

Faith, gentlemen, now I play a merchant's part,
And venture madly on a desperate mart.
BAPTISTA, to Gremio and Tranio,
The Taming of the Shrew, II, i

Shipwrights, whose sore task
Does not divide the Sunday from the week
MARCELLUS, to Horatio, *Hamlet*, I, i

Throw Physic to the Dogs: Medicine

Physicians are only incidental characters in Shakespeare's plays, and the only one to achieve a miraculous cure is already dead – Helena's father in *All's Well That Ends Well*, who on his deathbed leaves to her secret prescriptions with which she is able to cure the King of France. In *Cymbeline*, the doctor, Cornelius, although a minor character, plays an important part in the plot by substituting a sleeping draught for a lethal poison. In *The Merry Wives of Windsor*, there is Dr Caius, the French physician, whose profession is incidental to his role of blustering foreigner who entertains the audience with his rendering of the English language. Although Shakespeare shows some knowledge of medicine in that, for instance, he mentions Galen and Paracelsus, on the whole he makes little mention of the science. Apothecaries – the pharmacists of his day – were useful to his plots mostly as a source of poisons.

Give me an ounce of civet, good apothecary, to sweeten my imagination: there's money for thee.

LEAR, *King Lear*, IV, vi

Give me some drink; and bid the apothecary
Bring the strong poison that I bought of him.
CARDINAL BEAUFORT, *King Henry VI, Part 2*, III, iii

O true apothecary!
Thy drugs are quick.

ROMEO, *Romeo and Juliet*, V, iii

They are – he dies.

This young gentlewoman had a father . . . whose skill was almost as great as his honesty; had it stretched so far, would have made nature immortal, and death should have play for lack of work. Would, for the king's sake, he were living! I think it would be the death of the king's disease.
THE COUNTESS, of Helena's late father,
All's Well That Ends Well, I, i

[34]

Trust not the physician;
His antidotes are poison, and he slays
Moe than you rob.

TIMON, to bandits, *Timon of Athens*, IV, iii

The patient dies while the physician sleeps.

The Rape of Lucrece

COUNTESS: What hope is there of his majesty's amendment?
LAFEU: He hath abandoned his physicians, madam.

All's Well That Ends Well, I, i

He and his physicians
Are of a mind; he, that they cannot help him,
They, that they cannot help.

THE COUNTESS, to Helena, of the King,
All's Well That Ends Well, I, i

With the help of a surgeon he might yet recover, and
prove an ass.

THESEUS, *A Midsummer Night's Dream*, V, i

*On the death of Pyramus as performed by Bottom. Theseus
does not know that, earlier, Bottom had an ass's head.*

[35]

Now put it, God, in the physician's mind
To help him to his grave immediately!
RICHARD II, alluding to John of Gaunt,
Richard II, I, iv

As testy sick men, when their deaths be near,
No news but health from their physicians know.
SONNET CXL

If he were living, I would try him yet.
. . . the rest have worn me out
With several applications; nature and sickness
Debate it at their leisure.
THE KING, All's Well That Ends Well, I, ii

Thou speak'st like a physician, Helicanus,
That minister'st a potion unto me
That thou wouldst tremble to receive thyself.
PERICLES, Pericles, I, ii

Kill thy physician, and the fee bestow
Upon thy foul disease.
KENT, King Lear, I, i

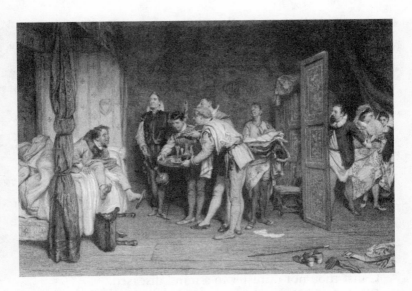

Your honour's players, hearing your amendment,
Are come to play a pleasant comedy;
For so your doctors hold it very meet,
Seeing too much sadness hath congeal'd your blood,
And melancholy is the nurse of frenzy:
Therefore they thought it good you hear a play
And frame your mind to mirth and merriment,
Which bars a thousand harms and lengthens life.

MESSENGER, to Christopher Sly,
The Taming of the Shrew, Induction, ii

Sly, a drunken tinker, is the subject of a practical joke. The local landowner, finding him asleep, has him transported to his home and dressed in fine clothes – when Sly wakes up, he is determinedly treated as a nobleman. Illness is blamed for his confusion, a recommended 'cure' being for him to watch a comedy – that 'pleasant comedy' is The Taming of the Shrew.

PAGE: I think you know him, Master Doctor Caius, the renowned French physician.

SIR HUGH EVANS: He has no more knowledge in Hibocrates and Galen, – and he is a knave besides; a cowardly knave as you would desires to be acquainted withal.

The Merry Wives of Windsor, III, i

As the doctor declares himself unable to cure Lady Macbeth with medicines, Macbeth asks him if he has some remedy for Scotland, something, perhaps, to purge the English from the land:

MACBETH:
Canst thou not minister to a mind diseased,
Pluck from the memory a rooted sorrow,
Raze out the written troubles of the brain
And with some sweet oblivious antidote
Cleanse the stuff'd bosom of that perilous stuff
Which weighs upon the heart?

DOCTOR:
Therein the patient
Must minister to himself.

MACBETH:
Throw physic to the dogs; I'll none of it . . .
If thou couldst, doctor, cast
The water of my land, find her disease,
And purge it to a sound and pristine health,
I would applaud thee to the very echo . . .
That should applaud again. – Pull't off, I say. –
What rhubarb, cyme, or what purgative drug,
Would scour these English hence?

Macbeth, V, iii

FALSTAFF: Sirrah, you giant, what says the doctor to my water?
PAGE: He said, sir, the water itself was a good healthy water;
   but, for the party that owed it, he might have more dis-
   eases than he knew for.

King Henry IV, Part 2, I, ii

Falstaff's page was very small.

CORDELIA: What can man's wisdom
   In the restoring his bereaved sense?
   He that helps him take all my outward worth.
DOCTOR: Our foster-nurse of nature is repose,
   The which he lacks.

King Lear, IV, iv

Who worse than a physician
Would this report become? But I consider,
By medicine life may be prolong'd, yet death
Will seize the doctor.

CYMBELINE, *Cymbeline,* V, v

*Cornelius, the doctor, has just told Cymbeline, the King, that the
Queen is dead. (He then goes on to tell the King what a
thoroughgoing baddie she actually was.)*

Storms of State: Politicians to Kings

Many of Shakespeare's plots turn on political issues; though, as he clearly recognized, it was advisable to steer clear of anything that could be seen as comment on the contemporary political situation. A good power struggle, however, forms a splendid basis for action. Kings murder, and are murdered for political power; Julius Caesar is assassinated because he shows signs of overweening ambition; indeed, ambition generally seems a challenge to the status quo, and the status quo is generally viewed as better than anything else on offer – would-be revolutionaries are shown as ignorant and possibly dangerous.

> Get thee glass eyes;
> And, like a scurvy politician, seem
> To see the things thou dost not.
>> LEAR, to Gloucester, *King Lear*, IV, vi
>
> *The Earl of Gloucester's eyes have been plucked out.*

> Equality of two domestic powers
> Breed scrupulous faction.
>> ANTONY, to Cleopatra, *Antony and Cleopatra*, I, iii

> An old man, broken with the storms of state.
>> GRIFFITH, to Katharine, of Cardinal Wolsey,
>> *King Henry VIII*, IV, ii

O, it is excellent
To have a giant's strength; but it is tyrannous
To use it like a giant.

> ISABELLA, to Angelo, *Measure for Measure,* II, ii

You speak o' the people,
As if you were a god to punish, not
A man of their infirmity.

> BRUTUS, to Coriolanus, *Coriolanus,* III, i

MENENIUS: The helms o' the state, who care for you like
fathers ...
FIRST CITIZEN: They ne'er cared for us yet: suffer us to
famish, and their store-houses crammed with grain; make
edicts for usury, to support usurers; repeal daily any
wholesome act established against the rich, and provide
more piercing statutes daily, to chain up and restrain the
poor. If the wars eat us not up, they will; and there's all the
love they bear us.

> *Coriolanus,* I, i

... My crown is call'd content;
A crown it is that seldom kings enjoy.

> HENRY VI, to two keepers,
> *King Henry VI, Part 3,* III, i

It is not to last much longer – and neither is he.

Kings are earth's gods; in vice their law's their will;
And if Jove stray, who dares say Jove doth ill?

PERICLES, to Antiochus, *Pericles*, I, i

MENENIUS: There was a time when all the body's members
  Rebell'd against the belly, thus accused it:
  That only like a gulf it did remain
  I' the midst o' the body, idle and unactive,
  Still cupboarding the viand, never bearing
  Like labour with the rest, where the other instruments
  Did see and hear, devise, instruct, walk, feel,
  And, mutually participate, did minister
  Unto the appetite and affection common
  Of the whole body. The belly answer'd – . . .
  . . . Note me this, good friend;
  Your most grave belly was deliberate,
  Not rash like his accusers, and thus answer'd:
  'True is it, my incorporate friends,' quoth he,
  'That I receive the general food at first,
  Which you do live upon; and fit it is,
  Because I am the store-house and the shop
  Of the whole body: but, if you do remember,
  I send it through the rivers of your blood,
  Even to the court, the heart, to the seat o' the brain;
  And, through the cranks and offices of man,
  The strongest nerves and small inferior veins
  From me receive that natural competency
  Whereby they live: and though that all at once,
  You, my good friends,' – this says the belly, 'mark me,' –
  . . . 'Though all at once cannot
  See what I do deliver out to each,
  Yet I can make my audit up, that all

From me do back receive the flour of all,
And leave me but the bran.' . . .
The senators of Rome are this good belly,
And you the mutinous members; for examine
Their counsels and their cares, digest things rightly
Touching the weal o' the common, you shall find
No public benefit which you receive
But it proceeds or comes from them to you
And no way from yourselves. What do you think,
You, the great toe of this assembly?
FIRST CITIZEN: I the great toe! why the great toe?

Coriolanus, I, i

*By the time Menenius, who draws out his body-politic metaphor
for as long as he can, to distract the rioting citizens, has finished,
news arrives that the citizens have been allowed their elected
tribunes, who will represent them before the Senate, followed
shortly after by the news that Rome was in imminent danger
of invasion from the Volsces.*

His will is not his own;
For he himself is subject to his birth:
He may not, as unvalued persons do,
Carve for himself; for on his choice depends
The safety and health of this whole state.

LAERTES, to Ophelia, *Hamlet*, I, iii

*Hamlet, as heir to the throne, may not do as he likes (specifically,
marry whom he wishes – that is, Ophelia), as the state comes first.*

What infinite heart's-ease
Must kings neglect, that private men enjoy!
And what have kings, that privates have not too,
Save ceremony, save general ceremony?
HENRY V, King Henry V, IV, i

Landlord of England art thou now, not king.
JOHN OF GAUNT, to Richard II, King Richard II, II, i

Hear him debate of commonwealth affairs,
You would say it hath been all in all his study.
THE ARCHBISHOP OF CANTERBURY,
to the Bishop of Ely, about the King,
King Henry V, I, i

The caterpillars of the commonwealth,
Which I have sworn to weed and pluck away.
HENRY BOLINGBROKE, to Lords,
King Richard II, II, iii

The caterpillars are Bushy, Bagot and their accomplices.

Civil dissension is a viperous worm
That gnaws the bowels of the commonwealth.
HENRY VI, to Lords, King Henry VI, Part 1, III, i

Therefore, my Harry,
Be it thy course to busy giddy minds
With foreign quarrels.

HENRY IV, to his son, *King Henry IV, Part 2*, IV, v

CADE: Be brave, then; for your captain is brave, and vows
reformation. There shall be in England seven halfpenny
loaves sold for a penny: the three-hooped pot shall have
ten hoops and I will make it felony to drink small beer: all
the realm shall be in common; and in Cheapside shall my
palfrey go to grass: and when I am king, as king I will be, –
ALL: God save your majesty!
CADE: I thank you, good people: there shall be no money;
all shall eat and drink on my score; and I will apparel
them all in one livery, that they may agree like brothers
and worship me their lord.

King Henry IV, Part 2, IV, ii

*Jack Cade is not advocating temperance, but, rather, strong as
opposed to weak beer. His plans for an England under his rule
had a few flaws . . .*

BRABANTIO: Thou art a villain.
IAGO: You are – a senator.

Othello, I, i

A politician . . . one that would circumvent God.

HAMLET, *Hamlet*, V, i

[45]

Uneasy lies the head that wears a crown.
HENRY IV, *King Henry IV, Part 2*, III, i

How sweet a thing it is to wear a crown;
Within whose circuit is Elysium
And all that poets feign of bliss and joy.
RICHARD, to his father, the Duke of York,
King Henry IV, Part 3, I, ii

Richard is to become Richard III.

This vile politician.
HOTSPUR, to Northumberland,
King Henry IV, Part 1, I, iii

The 'politician' in question is Bolingbroke – Henry IV.

For how can tyrants safely govern home,
Unless abroad they purchase great alliance?
QUEEN MARGARET, *King Henry VI, Part 3*, III, iii

When Mercy Seasons Justice: the Law, Justice and Mercy

As a humanist, Shakespeare believed in justice, but generally a justice tempered by mercy and compassion (where dramatically expedient in his plays). Although there are numerous references throughout his work to the law and lawyers, they are not often the butt of any wicked humour. Lawyers numbered among his friends, and he didn't want to kill them, whatever he might have thought of the fees they charged – but he recognized that the law had its faults: it could in some instances be 'bought out', as King Claudius remarks, or be misused or over-harsh; that lawyers might use 'tricks' or confuse people with legal niceties – their quillets and quiddities.

Old father antick the law.

FALSTAFF, *King Henry IV, Part 1*, I, ii

The first thing we do, let's kill all the lawyers.

DICK THE BUTCHER, *King Henry VI, Part 2*, IV, ii

Sir Hugh, persuade me not; I will make a Star-chamber matter of it: if he were twenty Sir John Falstaffs, he shall not abuse Robert Shallow, esquire.

JUSTICE SHALLOW, *The Merry Wives of Windsor*, I, i

Unless my study and my books be false,
The argument you held was wrong in you:

LAWYER, *King Henry VI, Part 1*, II, ii

For who would bear . . . the law's delay.

HAMLET, *Hamlet*, III, i

*One of a list of many tribulations that together seem to him a
good reason for doing away with oneself.*

In law, what plea so tainted and corrupt
But, being season'd with a gracious voice,
Obscures the show of evil?

BASSANIO, *The Merchant of Venice*, III, ii

In the corrupted currents of this world
Offence's gilded hand may shove by justice,
And oft 'tis seen the wicked prize itself
Buys out the law: but 'tis not so above;
There is no shuffling, there the action lies
In his true nature; and we ourselves compell'd,
Even to the teeth and forehead of our faults,
To give in evidence.

CLAUDIUS, *Hamlet*, III, iii

Heaven is above all yet; there sits a judge
That no king can corrupt.

KATHARINE, *Henry VIII*, III, i

Why may not that be the skull of a lawyer? Where be his quiddities now, his quillets, his cases, his tenures, and his tricks?

HAMLET, in the graveyard, *Hamlet*, V, i

Between two hawks, which flies the higher pitch;
Between two dogs, which hath the deeper mouth;
Between two blades, which bears the better temper:
Between two horses, which doth bear him best;
Between two girls, which hath the merriest eye;
I have perhaps some shallow spirit of judgement;
But in these nice sharp quillets of the law,
Good faith, I am no wiser than a daw.

THE EARL OF WARWICK, *Henry VI, Part 1*, II, iv

The law, which is past depth
To those that, without heed, do plunge into't.

ALCIBIADES, to two Senators, *Timon of Athens*, III, v

Use every man after his desert, and who should 'scape whipping?

HAMLET, disillusioned, to Polonius, *Hamlet*, II, ii

[49]

He hath ribbons of all the colours i' the rainbow; points
more than all the lawyers in Bohemia can learnedly
handle, though they come to him by the gross . . .

SERVANT, to the Clown and Polixenes,
The Winter's Tale, IV, iv

The pedlar he describes is Autolycus.

Crack the lawyer's voice,
That he may never more false title plead,
Nor sound his quillets shrilly.

TIMON, Timon of Athens, IV, iii

O, then, I see Queen Mab hath been with you.
And in this state she gallops night by night . . .
O'er lawyers' fingers, who straight dream on fees.

MERCUTIO, to Romeo, Romeo and Juliet, I, iv

KENT: This is nothing, fool.
FOOL: Then 'tis like the breath of an unfee'd lawyer; you
gave me nothing for't.

King Lear, I, iv

*The Fool has just recited a short homily to King Lear, which
Kent dismisses as 'nothing'.*

Though we are justices and doctors and churchmen,
Master Page, we have some salt of our youth in us; we are
the sons of women, Master Page.
JUSTICE SHALLOW, *The Merry Wives of Windsor*, II, iii

The laws, your curb and whip, in their rough power
Have uncheque'd theft.
TIMON, to a group of surprised thieves,
Timon of Athens, IV, iii

The justice,
In fair round belly with good capon lined,
With eyes severe and beard of formal cut,
Full of wise saws and modern instances.
JAQUES, *As You Like It*, II, vii

When law can do no right,
Let it be lawful that law bar no wrong.
CONSTANCE, *King John*, III, i

Thou hast appointed justices of peace, to call poor men
before them about matters they were not able to answer.
JACK CADE, *King Henry VI, Part 2*, IV, vii

Is not this a lamentable thing, that of the skin of an innocent lamb should be made parchment? that parchment, being scribbled o'er, should undo a man?

JACK CADE, *King Henry VI, Part 2*, IV, ii

Parchment was used for legal documents.

Still you keep o' th' windy side of the law.

FABIAN, to Sir Toby Belch, *Twelfth Night*, III, iv

Well, Time is the old justice that examines all such offenders.

ROSALIND, to Orlando, *As You Like It*, IV, i

'Such offenders' being those who fail to keep assignations on time, as promised.

A man may see how this world goes with no eyes. Look with thine ears: see how yond justice rails upon yon simple thief. Hark, in thine ear: change places; and, handy-dandy, which is the justice, which is the thief?

LEAR, to the blinded Gloucester, *King Lear*, IV, vi

Let the law go whistle.

CLOWN, to the Shepherd, *The Winter's Tale*, IV, iv

And do as adversaries do in law,
Strive mightily, but eat and drink as friends.

TRANIO, to Grumio and Biondello,
The Taming of the Shrew, I, ii

*The servants of rival suitors for the hand of Katharina's sister
Bianca; they are friends but are working on behalf of rivals.*

The bloody book of law
You shall yourself read in the bitter letter
After your own sense.

THE DUKE OF VENICE, to Brabantio, *Othello*, I, iii

*Brabantio has just claimed that his daughter, Desdemona, has
been abused, corrupted, stolen by witchcraft . . .*

The jury, passing on the prisoner's life,
May in the sworn twelve have a thief or two
Guiltier than him they try.

ANGELO, *Measure for Measure*, II, i

And what makes robbers bold but too much lenity?

CLIFFORD, *King Henry VI, Part 3*, II, vi

*In a dying speech, he regrets that the king had not been more
forceful in keeping his enemies down.*

Nothing emboldens sin so much as mercy.

FIRST SENATOR, *Timon of Athens*, III, v

We have strict statutes and most biting laws.
Having bound up the threatening twigs of birch,
Only to stick it in their children's sight
For terror, not to use, in time the rod
Becomes more mock'd than fear'd;
And liberty plucks justice by the nose;
The baby beats the nurse, and quite athwart
Goes all decorum.

DUKE VINCENTIO, to Friar Thomas,
Measure for Measure, I, iii

The Duke admits that he has been somewhat lax in enforcing the law.

We must not make a scarecrow of the law,
Setting it up to fear the birds of prey,
And let it keep one shape, till custom make it
Their perch and not their terror.

ANGELO, to Escalus, *Measure for Measure*, II, i

Angelo, entrusted by the Duke to exercise power in his absence, is overzealous in his enforcement of the law.

The law hath not been dead, though it hath slept.

ANGELO, to Isabella, *Measure for Measure*, II, ii

No ceremony that to great ones 'longs,
Not the king's crown, nor the deputed sword,
The marshal's truncheon, nor the judge's robe,
Become them with one half so good a grace
As mercy does.

ISABELLA, to Angelo,
Measure for Measure, II, ii

Sweet mercy is nobility's true badge.

TAMORA, to Titus,
Titus Andronicus, I, i

*Titus does not show mercy to her son, and the vengeance she
exacts is bloody and merciless.*

The law I bear no malice for my death;
'T has done, upon the premises, but justice:
But those that sought it I could wish more Christians.

THE DUKE OF BUCKINGHAM, *Henry VIII*, II, i

Forbear to judge, for we are sinners all.
Close up his eyes, and draw the curtain close;
And let us all to meditation.

HENRY VI, of Cardinal Beaufort,
King Henry VI, Part 2, III, iii

*Henry Beaufort has just died, delirious and apparently confessing
to involvement in a murder.*

... pity is the virtue of the law,
And none but tyrants use it cruelly.

ALCIBIADES to two Senators, *Timon of Athens*, III, v

The quality of mercy is not strain'd,
It droppeth as the gentle rain from heaven
Upon the place beneath: it is twice bless'd;
It blesseth him that gives and him that takes:
'Tis mightiest in the mightiest; it becomes
The throned monarch better than his crown;
His sceptre shows the force of temporal power,
The attribute to awe and majesty,
Wherein doth sit the dread and fear of kings;
But mercy is above this sceptred sway,
It is enthroned in the hearts of kings,
It is an attribute to God himself,
And earthly power doth then show likest God's
When mercy seasons justice. Therefore, Jew,
Though justice be thy plea, consider this,
That in the course of justice none of us
Should see salvation: we do pray for mercy,
And that same prayer doth teach us all to render
The deeds of mercy.

PORTIA, *The Merchant of Venice*, IV, i

*The tone of Portia's justly famous speech, uttered in the guise of a
young lawyer, 'Balthasar', is deceptively gentle. When she fails to
persuade Shylock to show mercy, and has led him on to believe
that the law shall prevail, she poses the condition (a wickedly
witty ruse?): he may take his pound of flesh – but if a drop of
blood is spilt, he loses his land and goods.*

Full of Strange Oaths: The Military

Soldiers appear in many of the historical plays and tragedies, as minor characters necessary to move the action on, as messengers or to comment on what is happening. Or – as Falstaff comments of his ragged band – as cannon fodder. Then there are the higher-ranking soldiers – Iago, Macbeth, Antony – men whose ambition proves their undoing.

Th'unconsidered soldier.
>> ARCITE to Palamon, *Two Noble Kinsmen*, I, ii

Then a soldier,
Full of strange oaths and bearded like the pard,
Jealous in honour, sudden and quick in quarrel,
Seeking the bubble reputation
Even in the cannon's mouth.
>> JAQUES, *As You Like It*, II, vii

That in the captain's but a choleric word,
Which in the soldier is flat blasphemy.
>> ISABELLA, to Angelo, *Measure for Measure*, II, ii

Thou art a soldier, therefore seldom rich.
>> TIMON, to Alcibiades, *Timon of Athens*, I, ii

If I be not ashamed of my soldiers, I am a soused gurnet
... my whole charge consists of ancients, corporals,
lieutenants, gentlemen of companies, slaves as ragged as
Lazarus in the painted cloth, where the glutton's dogs
licked his sores; and such as indeed were never soldiers,
but discarded unjust serving-men, younger sons to
younger brothers, revolted tapsters and ostlers trade-
fallen, the cankers of a calm world and a long peace.

FALSTAFF, King Henry IV, Part 1, IV, ii

Let no soldier fly.
He that is truly dedicate to war
Hath no self-love, nor he that loves himself
Hath not essentially but by circumstance
The name of valour.

YOUNG CLIFFORD, King Henry VI, Part 2, V, ii

All furnish'd, all in arms;
All plumed like estridges that with the wind
Baited like eagles having lately bathed;
Glittering in golden coats, like images;
As full of spirit as the month of May,
And gorgeous as the sun at midsummer;
Wanton as youthful goats, wild as young bulls.

VERNON, to Hotspur, King Henry IV, Part 1, I, iii

A description of Prince Henry and his men.

Food for powder, food for powder; they'll fill a pit as well as better: tush, man, mortal men, mortal men.

FALSTAFF, to Prince Henry,
King Henry IV, Part 1, IV, ii

I am a soldier, and unapt to weep,
Or to exclaim on fortune's fickleness.

REIGNIER, to Suffolk,
King Henry VI, Part 1, V, iii

You may relish him more in the soldier than in the scholar.

CASSIO, to Desdemona, of Iago, *Othello*, II, i

He's a soldier, and for one to say a soldier lies, is stabbing.

CLOWN, to Desdemona, *Othello*, III, iv

*Desdemona has just asked where Cassio 'lies', meaning 'resides';
the Clown pretends to mistake her meaning.*

Fie, my lord, fie! a soldier, and afeard?

LADY MACBETH, *Macbeth*, V, i

*Lady Macbeth is sleepwalking, her speech rambling. Her confused
mind has returned to the time she was spurring her husband to
murder Duncan.*

A soldier's a man;
A life's but a span;
Why, then, let a soldier drink.

IAGO, *Othello*, II, iii

ANTONY: Thou art a soldier only: speak no more.
ENOBARBUS: That truth should be silent I had almost forgot.

Antony and Cleopatra, II, ii

This Great Stage of Fools: Acting

To Shakespeare – actor and playwright – the stage was an essential part of life, and a favourite metaphor of his was the world as theatre – *As You Like It, King Lear, Macbeth, The Merchant of Venice, Richard II, The Tempest*, especially, refer to the world as a stage, its denizens as players. There are also some pointers to Shakespeare's view of the art of drama – particularly interesting in that he clearly did not care for histrionic acting or noisy melodramatics.

All the world's a stage,
And all the men and women merely players:
They have their exits and their entrances.

JAQUES, As You Like It, II, vii

The best actors in the world, either for tragedy, comedy, history, pastoral, pastoral-comical, historical-pastoral, tragical-historical, tragical-comical-historical-pastoral, scene individable, or poem unlimited.

> POLONIUS, announcing the newly arrived actors to Hamlet, *Hamlet*, II, ii

BOTTOM: Let me play the lion too: I will roar, that I will do any man's heart good to hear me; I will roar . . .

QUINCE: An you should do it too terribly, you would fright the duchess and the ladies . . .

BOTTOM: I will aggravate my voice so that I will roar you as gently as any sucking dove; I will roar you an 'twere any nightingale.

QUINCE: You can play no part but Pyramus . . .

BOTTOM: What beard were I best to play it in? . . .
I will discharge it in either your straw-colour beard, your orange-tawny beard, your purple-in-grain beard, or your French-crown-colour beard, your perfect yellow.

> *A Midsummer Night's Dream*, I, ii

As in a theatre, the eyes of men,
After a well-grac'd actor leaves the stage,
Are idly bent on him that enters next,
Thinking his prattle to be tedious.

> DUKE OF YORK, *King Richard II*, V, ii

When we are born, we cry that we are come
To this great stage of fools.

KING LEAR, *King Lear*, IV, vi

Suit the action to the word, the word to the action; with
this special observance, that you o'erstep not the modesty
of nature.

HAMLET, *Hamlet*, III, ii

That will ask some tears in the true performing of it:
if I do it, let the audience look to their eyes; I will move
storms, I will condole in some measure. To the rest: yet
my chief humour is for a tyrant: I could play Ercles rarely,
or a part to tear a cat in, to make all split . . . This is
Ercles' vein, a tyrant's vein; a lover is more condoling.

BOTTOM, A *Midsummer Night's Dream*, I, ii

Assessing the part he is to play in the 'lamentable comedy',
Pyramus and Thisby *('Ercles' is Hercules).*

Life's but a walking shadow, a poor player
That struts and frets his hour upon the stage
And then is heard no more: it is a tale
Told by an idiot, full of sound and fury,
Signifying nothing.

MACBETH, *Macbeth*, V, v

The quick comedians
Extemporally will stage us, and present
Our Alexandrian revels. Antony
Shall be brought drunken forth, and I shall see
Some squeaking Cleopatra boy my greatness
I' the posture of a whore.

CLEOPATRA, *Antony and Cleopatra*, V, ii

Musing on how their story would be played on stage, with a young boy playing her part.

Speak the speech, I pray you, as I pronounced it to you,
trippingly on the tongue; but if you mouth it, as many of
your players do, I had as lief the towncrier spoke my lines.
Nor do not saw the air too much with your hand, thus;
but use all gently: for in the very torrent, tempest, and – as
I may say – whirlwind of passion, you must acquire and
beget a temperance, that may give it smoothness. O! it
offends me to the soul to hear a robustious periwig-pated
fellow tear a passion to tatters, to very rags, to split the
ears of the groundlings, who for the most part are capable
of nothing but inexplicable dumb-shows and noise: I
would have such a fellow whipped for o'erdoing
Termagant; it out-herods Herod.

HAMLET, lecturing the actors, *Hamlet*, III, ii

They are the abstract and brief chronicles of the time.

HAMLET, of the actors, to Polonius, *Hamlet*, I, ii

Like a dull actor now,
I have forgot my part.

CORIOLANUS, *Coriolanus*, V, ii

I hold the world but as the world, Gratiano;
A stage where every man must play a part,
And mine a sad one.

ANTONIO, *The Merchant of Venice*, I, i

But do not like to stage me to their eyes:
Through it do well, I do not relish well
Their loud applause and Aves vehement;
Nor do I think the man of safe discretion
That does affect it.

DUKE VINCENTIO, to Angelo, *Measure For Measure*, I, i

Like a strutting player, whose conceit
Lies in his hamstring, and doth think it rich
To hear the wooden dialogue and sound
'Twixt his stretch'd footing and the scaffoldage.

ULYSSES, *Troilus and Cressida*, I, iii

No epilogue, I pray you; for your play needs no excuse.
Never excuse.

THESEUS, *A Midsummer's Night Dream*, V, i

Thus play I in one person many people,
And none contented: sometimes am I king;
Then treasons make me wish myself a beggar,
And so I am: then crushing penury
Persuades me I was better when a king;
Then am I king'd again: and by and by
Think that I am unking'd by Bolingbroke,
And straight am nothing: but whate'er I be,
Nor I nor any man that but man is
With nothing shall be pleased, till he be eased
With being nothing.

RICHARD II, *King Richard II*, V, i

*Imprisoned and alone, he considers peopling his 'little world'
by assuming different roles.*

GLOUCESTER:
Come, cousin, canst thou quake, and change thy colour,
Murder thy breath in the middle of a word,
And then begin again, and stop again,
As if thou wert distraught and mad with terror?
BUCKINGHAM:
Tut, I can counterfeit the deep tragedian;
Speak and look back, and pry on every side,
Tremble and start at wagging of a straw,
Intending deep suspicion: ghastly looks
Are at my service, like enforced smiles;
And both are ready in their offices,
At any time, to grace my stratagems.

King Richard III, III, v

How many ages hence
Shall this our lofty scene be acted over
In states unborn and accents yet unknown!

CASSIUS, to Brutus, *Julius Caesar*, III, i

'Tis ten to one this play can never please
All that are here: some come to take their ease,
And sleep an act or two; but those, we fear,
We have frighted with our trumpets; so, 'tis clear,
They'll say 'tis naught: others, to hear the city
Abused extremely, and to cry 'That's witty!'
Which we have not done neither: that, I fear,
All the expected good we're like to hear
For this play at this time, is only in
The merciful construction of good women;
For such a one we show'd 'em: if they smile,
And say 'twill do, I know, within a while
All the best men are ours; for 'tis ill hap,
If they hold when their ladies bid 'em clap.

King Henry VIII, Epilogue

Our revels now are ended. These our actors,
As I foretold you, were all spirits and
Are melted into air, into thin air:
And, like the baseless fabric of this vision,
The cloud-capp'd towers, the gorgeous palaces,
The solemn temples, the great globe itself,
Yea, all which it inherit, shall dissolve
And, like this insubstantial pageant faded,
Leave not a rack behind. We are such stuff
As dreams are made on, and our little life
Is rounded with a sleep.

PROSPERO, *The Tempest*, IV, i

Exit, pursued by a bear.

The Winter's Tale, III, iii

The most famous stage direction in the English language.

[68]

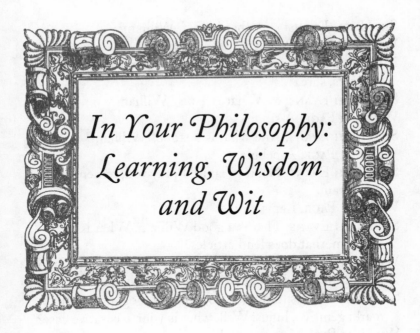

In Your Philosophy:
Learning, Wisdom
and Wit

LEARNING, in the sense of formal schooling, is perhaps not taken that seriously in Shakespeare's work, although, as is clear from Jack Cade's speech (see below), he supported the idea of schools; on the other hand, both book-learning and wisdom are viewed as an important part of life, while wit, in its every sense, is of course essential to his plays.

... the whining school-boy, with his satchel
And shining morning face, creeping like snail
Unwillingly to school.

JAQUES, *As You Like It*, II, vii

SIR HUGH EVANS: . . .What is 'fair', William?

WILLIAM PAGE: Pulcher.

MISTRESS QUICKLY: Polecats! there are fairer things than polecats, sure.

SIR HUGH EVANS: . . .What is 'lapis,' William?

WILLIAM PAGE: A stone.

SIR HUGH EVANS: And what is 'a stone,' William?

WILLIAM PAGE: A pebble.

SIR HUGH EVANS: No, it is 'lapis:' I pray you, remember in your prain.

WILLIAM PAGE: Lapis.

SIR HUGH EVANS: That is a good William. What is he, William, that does lend articles?

WILLIAM PAGE: Articles are borrowed of the pronoun, and be thus declined, Singulariter, nominativo, hic, hæc, hoc.

SIR HUGH EVANS: Nominativo, hig, hag, hog; pray you, mark: genitivo, hujus. Well, what is your accusative case?

WILLIAM PAGE: Accusativo, hinc.

SIR HUGH EVANS: I pray you, have your remembrance, child, accusative, hung, hang, hog.

MISTRESS QUICKLY: 'Hang-hog' is Latin for bacon, I warrant you.

SIR HUGH EVANS: Leave your prabbles, 'oman. What is the focative case, William?

WILLIAM PAGE: O, – vocativo, O.

SIR HUGH EVANS: Remember, William; focative is caret.

MISTRESS QUICKLY: And that's a good root.

SIR HUGH EVANS: 'Oman, forbear.

MISTRESS QUICKLY: Peace!

SIR HUGH EVANS: What is your genitive case plural, William?

WILLIAM PAGE: Genitive case!

SIR HUGH EVANS: Ay.

WILLIAM PAGE: Genitive, – horum, harum, horum.

MISTRESS QUICKLY: Vengeance of Jenny's case! fie on her! never name her, child, if she be a whore.

SIR HUGH EVANS: For shame, 'oman.

MISTRESS QUICKLY: You do ill to teach the child such words: he teaches him to hick and to hack, which they'll do fast enough of themselves, and to call 'horum:' fie upon you!

The Merry Wives of Windsor, IV, i

Love goes toward love, as schoolboys from their books,
But love from love, toward school with heavy looks.

ROMEO, *Romeo and Juliet*, II, ii

Study is like the heaven's glorious sun,
That will not be deep-searched with saucy looks;
Small have continual plodders ever won,
Save base authority from others' books.

BEROWNE, *Love's Labour's Lost*, I, i

Thou hast most traitorously corrupted the youth of the realm in erecting a grammar school; and whereas, before, our forefathers had no other books but the score and the tally, thou hast caused printing to be used; and, contrary to the king, his crown, and dignity, thou hast built a paper-mill. It will be proved to thy face that thou hast men about thee that usually talk of a noun and a verb, and such abominable words as no Christian ear can endure to hear.

JACK CADE, *King Henry VI, Part 2*, IV, vii

You two are book-men.

DULL, Love's Labour's Lost, IV, ii

Glad that you thus continue your resolve
To suck the sweets of sweet philosophy.
Only, good master, while we do admire
This virtue and this moral discipline,
Let's be no stoics nor no stocks, I pray;
Or so devote to Aristotle's cheques
As Ovid be an outcast quite abjured:
Balk logic with acquaintance that you have
And practise rhetoric in your common talk;
Music and poesy use to quicken you;
The mathematics and the metaphysics,
Fall to them as you find your stomach serves you;
No profit grows where is no pleasure ta'en:
In brief, sir, study what you most affect.

TRANIO, The Taming of the Shrew, I, i

The guards are relieved to be able to hand over the task
of dealing with a ghost:

Thou art a scholar; speak to it, Horatio.

MARCELLUS, Hamlet, I, i

The fool doth think he is wise, but the wise man knows
himself to be a fool.

TOUCHSTONE, As You Like It, V, i

Malvolio has been pronounced mad and locked up in a dark room; his complaints are met with teasing:

I say there is no darkness but ignorance, in which thou art more puzzled than the Egyptians in their fog.

FESTE, the Clown, *Twelfth Night*, IV, ii

It is a good divine that follows his own instructions: I can easier teach twenty what were good to be done, than be one of the twenty to follow mine own teaching.

PORTIA, *The Merchant of Venice*, I, ii

Within the book and volume of my brain.

HAMLET, *Hamlet*, I, v

To be a well-favoured man is the gift of fortune; but to write and read comes by nature.

DOGBERRY, *Much Ado About Nothing*, III, iii

While memory holds a seat
In this distracted globe. Remember thee!
Yea, from the table of my memory
I'll wipe away all trivial fond records.

HAMLET, *Hamlet*, I, v

I'll note you in my book of memory.
RICHARD PLANTAGENET, *King Henry VI, Part 1*, II, iv

SNUG: Have you the lion's part written? pray you, if it be, give it me, for I am slow of study.
QUINCE: You may do it extempore, for it is nothing but roaring.
A Midsummer Night's Dream, I, ii

I never knew so young a body with so old a head.
BELLARIO, *The Merchant of Venice*, IV, i

In his letter of recommendation of Balthasar, a young 'doctor of laws' – Portia in disguise.

They have a plentiful lack of wit.
HAMLET, *Hamlet*, II, ii

Polonius has asked Hamlet what he is reading about: 'Slanders, sir: for the satirical rogue says here that old men have grey beards, that their faces are wrinkled . . .'

MESSENGER: I see, lady, the gentleman is not in your books.
BEATRICE: No; an he were, I would burn my study.
Referring to Benedick, *Much Ado About Nothing*, I, i

There is a history in all men's lives.
WARWICK, *King Henry IV, Part 2*, III, i

I fear he will prove the weeping philosopher when he
grows old, being so full of unmannerly sadness in his
youth.
PORTIA, of one of her suitors, the County palatine,
The Merchant of Venice, I, ii

A good old man, sir; he will be talking: as they say, when
the age is in, the wit is out.
DOGBERRY, of Verges, *Much Ado About Nothing*, III, v

To expostulate . . . why day is day, night night, and time is
time, were nothing but to waste night, day, and time.
POLONIUS, *Hamlet*, II, ii

The brain of this foolish-compounded clay, man, is not
able to invent anything that tends to laughter, more than I
invent or is invented on me: I am not only witty in myself,
but the cause that wit is in other men.
FALSTAFF, *King Henry IV, Part 2*, I, ii

What, in thy quips and thy quiddities?
    FALSTAFF, to Prince Henry, *King Henry IV, Part 1*, I, ii

He's winding up the watch of his wit. By and by it will strike.
    SEBASTIAN, to Antonio, mocking Gonzalo,
        The Tempest, II, i

TOUCHSTONE: Hast any philosophy in thee, shepherd?
CORIN: No more but that I know the more one sickens the worse at ease he is; and that he that wants money, means and content is without three good friends; that the property of rain is to wet and fire to burn; that good pasture makes fat sheep, and that a great cause of the night is lack of the sun; that he that hath learned no wit by nature nor art may complain of good breeding or comes of a very dull kindred.
TOUCHSTONE: Such a one is a natural philosopher.
    As You Like It, III, ii

Your wit's too hot, it speeds too fast, 'twill tire.
    BEROWNE, to Rosaline, *Love's Labour's Lost*, II, i

There are more things in heaven and earth, Horatio,
Than are dreamt of in your philosophy.
    HAMLET, *Hamlet*, I, v

THIRD FISHERMAN: Master, I marvel how the fishes live in the sea.
FIRST FISHERMAN: Why, as men do a-land; the great ones eat up the little ones.

Pericles, II, i

. . . there was never yet philosopher
That could endure the toothache patiently.
LEONATO, *Much Ado About Nothing*, V, i

He doth indeed show some sparks that are like wit.
DON PEDRO, to Claudio, on Benedick,
Much Ado About Nothing, II, iii

Playing Upon the Word

As a tool of both his trades – writer and actor – words were of the utmost importance to Shakespeare, and he clearly derived great enjoyment from using them, relishing puns and other forms of word play. He delighted in giving his characters great ranting speeches and pithy one-liners, all of which served to manipulate the audience – drawing their attention, keeping them in suspense, catching at their sympathies – keeping them in 'a rhapsody of words'.

Out, idle words, servants to shallow fools,
Unprofitable sounds, weak arbitrators!
Busy yourselves in skill-contending schools,
Debate where leisure serves with dull debaters.

The Rape of Lucrece

[78]

What's in a name? that which we call a rose
By any other name would smell as sweet.

JULIET, Romeo and Juliet, II, ii

A good mouth-filling oath.

HOTSPUR, King Henry IV, Part 1, III, i

A rhapsody of words.

HAMLET, Hamlet, III, iv

Here will be an old abusing of God's patience and the
king's English.

MISTRESS QUICKLY, The Merry Wives of Windsor, I, iv

Dr Caius is arriving

How every fool can play upon the word! I think the best
grace of wit will shortly turn into silence, and discourse
grow commendable in none only but parrots.

LORENZO, The Merchant of Venice, III, v

Comparisons are odorous.

DOGBERRY, to Verges, Much Ado About Nothing, III, v

POLONIUS: What do you read, my lord?
HAMLET: Words, words, words.

Hamlet, II, ii

Words, words, mere words, no matter from the heart.

TROILUS, *Troilus and Cressida*, V, iii

MOTH: They have been at a great feast of languages, and
stolen the scraps.
COSTARD: O! they have lived long on the alms-basket of
words. I marvel thy master hath not eaten thee for a word;
for thou art not so long by the head as honorificabilitudin-
itatibus: thou art easier swallowed than a flap-dragon.

Love's Labour's Lost, V, i

He draweth out the thread of his verbosity finer than the
staple of his argument.

HOLOFERNES, of Adriano, *Love's Labour's Lost*, V, i

Shall quips and sentences and these paper bullets of the
brain awe a man from the career of his humour?

BENEDICK, *Much Ado About Nothing*, II, iii

My words fly up, my thoughts remain below:
Words without thoughts never to heaven go.

CLAUDIUS, Hamlet, III, iii

Words pay no debts.

PANDARUS, Troilus and Cressida, III, ii

Ferdinand, King of Navarre, has just decided to turn his court into 'a little academe', where all would devote their time to serious study – such frivolities as banqueting, general merry-making, and the company of women, are banned (the King has forgotten that the French King's daughter is expected at court as ambassador for her ill father: already an exception to his rules has to be made). Costard has been seen in company with Jaquenetta by a Spanish visitor at court, Don Adriano de Armado, a gentleman 'that hath a mint of phrases in his brain'. Here, Ferdinand opens and reads a magnificently wordy and orotund letter from Armado, counterpointed by Costard's comic interruptions.

'Great deputy, the welkin's vicegerent and sole dominator of
    Navarre, my soul's earth's god, and body's fostering
    patron.'
COSTARD: Not a word of Costard yet.
FERDINAND: [*Reads*] 'So it is,' –
COSTARD: It may be so: but if he say it is so, he is, in telling
    true, but so.
FERDINAND: Peace!
COSTARD: Be to me and every man that dares not fight!
FERDINAND: No words!

COSTARD: Of other men's secrets, I beseech you.

FERDINAND: [*Reads*] 'So it is, besieged with sable-coloured melancholy, I did commend the black-oppressing humour to the most wholesome physic of thy health-giving air; and, as I am a gentleman, betook myself to walk. The time when. About the sixth hour; when beasts most graze, birds best peck, and men sit down to that nourishment which is called supper: so much for the time when. Now for the ground which; which, I mean, I walked upon: it is y-cleped thy park. Then for the place where; where, I mean, I did encounter that obscene and preposterous event, that draweth from my snow-white pen the ebon-coloured ink, which here thou viewest, beholdest, surveyest, or seest; but to the place where; it standeth north-north-east and by east from the west corner of thy curious-knotted garden: there did I see that low-spirited swain, that base minnow of thy mirth,' –

COSTARD: Me?

FERDINAND: [*Reads*] 'that unlettered small-knowing soul,' –

COSTARD: Me?

FERDINAND: [*Reads*] 'that shallow vassal,' –

COSTARD: Still me?

FERDINAND: [*Reads*] 'which, as I remember, hight Costard,' –

COSTARD: O, me!

FERDINAND: [*Reads*] 'sorted and consorted, contrary to thy established proclaimed edict and continent canon, which with, – O, with – but with this I passion to say wherewith,' –

COSTARD: With a wench.

FERDINAND: [*Reads*] 'with a child of our grandmother Eve, a female; or, for thy more sweet understanding, a woman. Him I, as my ever-esteemed duty pricks me on, have sent to thee, to receive the meed of punishment, by thy sweet

grace's officer, Anthony Dull; a man of good repute,
carriage, bearing, and estimation.'
DULL: Me, an't shall please you.

Love's Labour's Lost, I, i

You taught me language; and my profit on 't
Is, I know how to curse: the red plague rid you,
For learning me your language!

CALIBAN, *The Tempest*, I, ii

This is most brave,
That I, the son of a dear father murdered,
Prompted to my revenge by heaven and hell,
Must, like a whore, unpack my heart with words,
And fall a-cursing, like a very drab.

HAMLET, *Hamlet*, II, ii

These are but wild and whirling words, my lord.

HORATIO, *Hamlet*, I, v

He was wont to speak plain and to the purpose, like
an honest man and a soldier; and now is he turned
orthography; his words are a very fantastical banquet,
just so many strange dishes.

BENEDICK, of Claudio, *Much Ado About Nothing*, II, iii

O Sir, we quarrel in print, by the book; as you have books for good manners: I will name you the degrees. The first, the Retort Courteous; the second, the Quip Modest; the third, the Reply Churlish; the fourth, the Reproof Valiant; the fifth, the Countercheck Quarrelsome; the sixth, the Lie with Circumstance; the seventh, the Lie Direct.

TOUCHSTONE, *As You Like It*, V, iv

Valentine, a gentleman of Verona and suitor to Silvia, and his foolish rival Thurio fire salvoes of words at each other.

SILVIA: Servant, you are sad.
VALENTINE: Indeed, madam, I seem so.
THURIO: Seem you that you are not?
VALENTINE: Haply I do.
THURIO: So do counterfeits.
VALENTINE: So do you.
THURIO: What seem I that I am not?
VALENTINE: Wise.
THURIO: What instance of the contrary?
VALENTINE: Your folly.
THURIO: And how quote you my folly?
VALENTINE: I quote it in your jerkin.
THURIO: My jerkin is a doublet.
VALENTINE: Well, then, I'll double your folly.
THURIO: How?
SILVIA: What, angry, Sir Thurio! do you change colour?
VALENTINE: Give him leave, madam; he is a kind of chameleon.
THURIO: That hath more mind to feed on your blood than live in your air.
VALENTINE: You have said, sir.

THURIO: Ay, sir, and done too, for this time.

VALENTINE: I know it well, sir; you always end ere you begin.

SILVIA: A fine volley of words, gentlemen, and quickly shot off.

VALENTINE: 'Tis indeed, madam; we thank the giver.

SILVIA: Who is that, servant?

VALENTINE: Yourself, sweet lady; for you gave the fire. Sir Thurio borrows his wit from your ladyship's looks, and spends what he borrows kindly in your company.

THURIO: Sir, if you spend word for word with me, I shall make your wit bankrupt.

VALENTINE: I know it well, sir; you have an exchequer of words and, I think, no other treasure to give your followers, for it appears by their bare liveries, that they live by your bare words.

The Two Gentlemen of Verona, II, iv

Taffeta phrases, silken terms precise,
Three-pil'd hyperboles, spruce affectation,
Figures pedantical.

BEROWNE, *Love's Labour's Lost*, V, ii

Charm ache with air and agony with words.

LEONATO, *Much Ado About Nothing*, V, i

I will speak daggers to her, but use none.

HAMLET, referring to Gertrude, *Hamlet*, III, ii

They that dally nicely with words may quickly make them
wanton.

> VIOLA, *Twelfth Night*, III, i

... not to crack the wind of the poor phrase,
Running it thus.

> POLONIUS, to Ophelia, apologizing for a pun,
> *Hamlet*, I, iii

Such fanatical phantasimes, such insociable and point-
devise companions; such rackers of orthography, as to
speak dout, fine, when he should say doubt; det, when he
should pronounce debt, – d, e, b, t, not d, e, t: he clepeth a
calf, cauf; half, hauf; neighbour vocatur nebour; neigh
abbreviated ne. This is abhominable, – which he would
call abbominable: it insinuateth me of insanie: anne
intelligis, domine? to make frantic, lunatic.

> HOLOFERNES, of Armado, *Love's Labour's Lost*, V, i

How long a time lies in one little word!

> HENRY BOLINGBROKE, *King Richard II*, I, iii

*The word is, presumably, 'six' – the king has just reduced his
banishment to six years from ten: fours years lie in the one word.*

Zounds! I was never so bethump'd with words
Since I first call'd my brother's father dad.
PHILIP THE BASTARD, *King John*, II, i

Who you are and what you would are out of my welkin,
I might say 'element', but the word is over-worn.
FESTE, the Clown, to Viola, *Twelfth Night*, III, I

My salad days,
When I was green in judgment: cold in blood.
CLEOPATRA, *Antony and Cleopatra*, I, v

Men of few words are the best men.
BOY, *King Henry V*, III, ii

Mincing poetry:
'Tis like the forc'd gait of a shuffling nag.
HOTSPUR, *King Henry IV, Part 1*, III, i

This is the very false gallop of verses.
TOUCHSTONE, *As You Like It*, III, ii

Devise, wit; write, pen; for I am for whole volumes in folio.

DON ADRIANO DE ARMADO,
Love's Labour's Lost, I, ii

Let there be gall enough in thy ink.

SIR TOBY BELCH, *Twelfth Night*, III, ii

An honest tale speeds best being plainly told.

QUEEN ELIZABETH,
King Richard III, IV, iv

I once did hold it, as our statists do,
A baseness to write fair.

HAMLET, *Hamlet*, V, ii

As Hamlet had once shared with statists – statesmen – the opinion that untidy and unclear handwriting was smart, he was able easily to replace the document ordering his death with one ordering that of its bearers.

There are a sort of men . . .
As who should say 'I am Sir Oracle,
And when I ope my lips let no dog bark!'

GRATIANO, *The Merchant of Venice*, I, i

Mend your speech a little,
Lest it may mar your fortunes.

LEAR, *King Lear*, I, i

I want that glib and oily art
To speak and purpose not.

CORDELIA, *King Lear*, I, i

CASSIUS: Did Cicero say any thing?
CASCA: Ay, he spoke Greek.
CASSIUS: To what effect?
CASCA: Nay, an I tell you that, I'll ne'er look you i' the face
again: but those that understood him smiled at one
another and shook their heads; but, for mine own part, it
was Greek to me.

Julius Caesar, I, ii

'Tis a kind of good deed to say well:
And yet words are no deeds.

HENRY VIII, to Cardinal Wolsey,
King Henry VIII, III, ii

A jest's prosperity lies in the ear
Of him that hears it, never in the tongue
Of him that makes it.

ROSALINE, *Love's Labour's Lost*, V, ii

Talkers are no good doers.

FIRST MURDERER, *King Richard III*, I, iii

Ill deeds are doubled with an evil word.

LUCIANA, *The Comedy of Errors*, III, ii

For I have neither wit, nor words, nor worth,
Action, nor utterance, nor the power of speech,
To stir men's blood.
> MARK ANTONY, addressing the citizens of Rome,
> *Julius Caesar*, III, ii

Well said: that was laid on with a trowel.
> CELIA, to Rosalind and Touchstone,
> *As You Like It*, I, ii

Speak to me as to thy thinkings,
As thou dost ruminate, and give thy worst of thoughts
The worst of words.
> OTHELLO, to Iago, *Othello*, III, iii

That man that hath a tongue, I say, is no man,
If with his tongue he cannot win a woman.
VALENTINE, *The Two Gentlemen of Verona*, III, i

Most radiant, exquisite and unmatchable beauty, – I pray
you, tell me if this be the lady of the house, for I never saw
her: I would be loath to cast away my speech, for besides
that it is excellently well penned, I have taken great pains
to con it.
VIOLA, *Twelfth Night*, I, v

*In the guise of Cesario, Viola has come to Olivia as an emissary
of Duke Orsino.*

I understand a fury in your words,
But not the words.
DESDEMONA, to Othello, *Othello*, IV, ii

Where words are scarce, they are seldom spent in vain
For they breathe truth that breathe their words in pain.
The dying words of JOHN OF GAUNT to
the Duke of York, *Richard II*, II, i

It is the disease of not listening, the malady of not
marking, that I am troubled withal.
FALSTAFF, *King Henry IV, Part 2*, I, ii

Most Toad-Spotted: Insults and Abuse

INVECTIVE, insults, words of abuse – all are in plentiful supply in Elizabethan and Jacobean drama. As a theatrical device, invective and harangues have a multiplicity of uses: great diatribe can set the scene; a tirade against a character leaves the audience in no doubt of how the relationship between two characters is to be viewed, though the outcome is only to be guessed at – continuing hatred, or reconciliation, even love?

And, of course, an exchange of lively insults provides comic relief. None of Shakespeare's plays is without some instances of verbal abuse – and very varied they are too, from very basic robust insults to subtle barbs – and collections of his insults have been published, while many Shakespeare websites include a webpage devoted to them.

This section comprises a comparatively small selection, chosen mainly for their verbal inventiveness, their colour and gusto, their sharpness or their wit.

You are not worth another word, else I'd call you knave.
LAFEU, *All's Well That Ends Well*, II, iii

The tartness of his face sours ripe grapes: when he walks, he moves like an engine, and the ground shrinks before his treading.
MENENIUS, on Marcius, *Coriolanus*, V, iv

You Banbury cheese!

BARDOLPH, to Slender,
The Merry Wives of Windsor, I, i

His intellect is not replenished; he is only an animal, only sensible in the duller parts.
SIR NATHANIEL, of Dull, *Love's Labour's Lost*, IV, ii

Four of his five wits went halting off, and now is the whole man governed with one.
BEATRICE, of Benedick, *Much Ado About Nothing*, I, i

Thou deboshed fish thou.
TRINCULO, addressing the man-monster Caliban,
The Tempest, III, ii

Though I am not naturally honest, I am so sometimes by chance.

AUTOLYCUS, being honest, *The Winter's Tale*, IV, iv

Why dost thou converse with that trunk of humours, that bolting-hutch of beastliness, that swollen parcel of dropsies, that huge bombard of sack, that stuffed cloak-bag of guts, that roasted Manningtree ox with the pudding in his belly, that reverend vice, that grey iniquity, that father ruffian, that vanity in years? Wherein is he good, but to taste sack and drink it? wherein neat and cleanly, but to carve a capon and eat it? wherein cunning, but in craft? wherein crafty, but in villainy? wherein villainous, but in all things? wherein worthy, but in nothing?

PRINCE HENRY (Hal) to Falstaff,
King Henry IV, Part 1, II, iv

The Prince is pretending to be his father, King Henry IV,
upbraiding his son for consorting with Falstaff; Falstaff
has taken the role of the Prince.

What! my dear Lady Disdain, are you yet living?

BENEDICK, to Beatrice, *Much Ado About Nothing*, I, i

I do wish thou wert a dog,
That I might love thee something.

TIMON, to Alcibiades, *Timon of Athens*, IV, iii

[95]

Thy head is as full of quarrels as an egg is full of meat, and yet thy head hath been beaten as addle as an egg for quarrelling.

MERCUTIO, to Benvolio, *Romeo and Juliet*, III, i

Gratiano speaks an infinite deal of nothing, more than any man in all Venice. His reasons are as two grains of wheat hid in two bushels of chaff: you shall seek all day ere you find them, and when you have them, they are not worth the search.

BASSANIO, *The Merchant of Venice*, I, i

The devil damn thee black, thou cream-faced loon! Where got'st thou that goose look?

MACBETH, to a messenger, *Macbeth*, V, iii

Thou lily-liver'd boy.

MACBETH, to that unhappy messenger again,
Macbeth, V, iii

Having flown over many knavish professions, he settled only in rogue.

AUTOLYCUS, anonymously, of himself,
The Winter's Tale, IV, iii

She hath more hair than wit, and more faults than hairs, and more wealth than faults.

SPEED, to Launce,
The Two Gentlemen of Verona, III, i

Launce has written a list of his girlfriend's qualities, and his friend Speed is adding faults to it; unsurprisingly, Launce is quick to latch onto the 'more wealth' bit.

He has not so much brain as earwax.
   THERSITES, of Agamemnon, *Troilus and Cressida*, V, i

Thou sodden-witted lord! thou hast no more brain than I have in mine elbows.

THERSITES, to Ajax, *Troilus and Cressida*, II, i

There's small choice in rotten apples.

HORTENSIO, discussing Katharina with Gremio,
The Taming of the Shrew, I, i

The complaints I have heard of you I do not all believe; 'tis my slowness that I do not, for I know you lack not folly to commit them, and have ability enough to make such knaveries yours.

COUNTESS, to the Clown,
All's Well That Ends Well, I, iii

I do desire we may be better strangers.

Orlando, to Jaques, *As You Like It*, III, ii

*In his furious and disgusted hatred of the self-serving Oswald,
steward of King Lear's daughter Goneril, the Earl of Kent gives
vent to his feelings in a splendid tirade, with interruptions from
the Duke of Cornwall:*

Kent: No marvel, you have so bestirred your valour. You
cowardly rascal, nature disclaims in thee: a tailor made
thee.

Cornwall: Thou art a strange fellow: a tailor make a man?

Kent: Ay, a tailor, sir: a stone-cutter or painter could not
have made him so ill, though he had been but two hours
at the trade.

He gets the bit between his teeth:

A knave; a rascal; an eater of broken meats; a base, proud,
shallow, beggarly, three-suited, hundred-pound, filthy,
worsted-stocking knave; a lily-livered, action-taking knave,
a whoreson, glass-gazing, super-serviceable finical rogue;
one-trunk-inheriting slave; one that wouldst be a bawd, in
way of good service, and art nothing but the composition
of a knave, beggar, coward, pandar, and the son and heir of
a mongrel bitch: one whom I will beat into clamorous
whining, if thou deniest the least syllable of thy addition.
. . . Thou whoreson zed! thou unnecessary letter!
. . . That such a slave as this should wear a sword,
Who wears no honesty. Such smiling rogues as these,
Like rats, oft bite the holy cords a-twain
Which are too intrinse t' unloose; smooth every passion
That in the natures of their lords rebel;

Bring oil to fire, snow to their colder moods;
Renege, affirm, and turn their halcyon beaks
With every gale and vary of their masters,
Knowing nought, like dogs, but following.

And, finally, irritated by the Duke of Cornwall's questions:

Sir, 'tis my occupation to be plain:
I have seen better faces in my time
Than stands on any shoulder that I see
Before me at this instant.

KENT, *King Lear*, II, ii

In his brain,
Which is as dry as the remainder biscuit
After a voyage, he hath strange places cramm'd
With observation, the which he vents
In mangled forms.

JAQUES, on Touchstone, *As You Like It*, II, vii

... My two schoolfellows,
Whom I will trust as I will adders fang'd.

HAMLET, referring to Rosencrantz and Guildenstern,
Hamlet, III, iv

And if his name be George, I'll call him Peter.

PHILIP THE BASTARD, *King John*, I, i

Asses are made to bear, and so are you.
KATHARINA, to Petruchio who has just invited her
to sit on him, *The Taming of the Shrew*, II, i

What cracker is this same that deafs our ears
With this abundance of superfluous breath?
AUSTRIA, referring to the Bastard, *King John*, II, i

Thy sin's not accidental, but a trade.
ISABELLA, to Claudio, *Measure For Measure*, III, i

His wit's as thick as Tewksbury mustard.
FALSTAFF, to Doll Tearsheet, of Poins,
King Henry IV, Part 1, II, iv

From the extremest upward of thy head
To the descent and dust below thy foot,
A most toad-spotted traitor.

> EDGAR, to his half-brother Edmund,
> *King Lear*, V, iii

He's a most notable coward, an infinite and endless liar, an hourly promise-breaker, the owner of no one good quality.

> SECOND LORD, to Bertram, of Parolles,
> *All's Well That Ends Well*, III, vi

PRINCE HENRY: .. this sanguine coward, this bed-presser, this horseback-breaker, this huge hill of flesh, –
FALSTAFF: 'Sblood, you starveling, you elf-skin, you dried neat's tongue, you bull's pizzle, you stock-fish! O for breath to utter what is like thee! you tailor's-yard, you sheath, you bowcase; you vile standing-tuck.

> *King Henry IV, Part 1*, II, iv

Your bum is the greatest thing about you; so that in the beastliest sense you are Pompey the Great.

> ESCALUS, to Pompey Bum, *Measure for Measure*, II, i

Falstaff, his bulk always the butt of jokes, is pleased to be able to retaliate at the expense of Bardolph's (a prototype Rudolph the Red-Nosed Reindeer?) nose:

BARDOLPH: Why, you are so fat, Sir John, that you must
    needs be out of all compass, out of all reasonable compass,
    Sir John.
FALSTAFF: Do thou amend thy face, and I'll amend my life:
    thou art our admiral, thou bearest the lantern in the poop,
    but 'tis in the nose of thee; thou art the Knight of the
    Burning Lamp.

                        King Henry IV, Part 1, III, iii

FIRST MURDERER: We are men, my liege.
MACBETH: Ay, in the catalogue ye go for men;
    As hounds and greyhounds, mongrels, spaniels, curs,
    Shoughs, water-rugs and demi-wolves, are clept
    All by the name of dogs.

                              Macbeth, III, i

Our very priests must become mockers, if they shall
encounter such ridiculous subjects as you are. When you
speak best unto the purpose, it is not worth the
wagging of your beards; and your beards deserve not so
honourable a grave as to stuff a botcher's cushion, or to be
entombed in an ass's pack-saddle . . . more of your
conversation would infect my brain.

                MENENIUS, addressing Brutus and Sicinius,
                          Coriolanus, II, i

Portia and Nerissa are discussing Portia's suitors:

NERISSA: What say you, then, to Falconbridge, the young
baron of England?
PORTIA: I think he bought his doublet in Italy, his round
hose in France, his bonnet in Germany and his behaviour
everywhere . . .
NERISSA: How say you by the French lord, Monsieur Le
Bon?
PORTIA: God made him, and therefore let him pass for a
man. In truth, I know it is a sin to be a mocker: but . . .
The Merchant of Venice, I, ii

I have heard of your paintings too, well enough; God hath
given you one face, and you make yourselves another: you
jig, you amble, and you lisp, and nickname God's
creatures, and make your wantonness your ignorance.
HAMLET, *Hamlet*, III, i

*Hamlet, in a combination of fury, disgust at all humanity
and at himself, and assumed madness, contrives to be as
unpleasant as he can be to the mild Ophelia.*

When all that is within him does condemn
Itself for being there.
MENTEITH, to Caithness, Angus and Lennox,
about Macbeth, *Macbeth*, V, ii

What tempest, I trow, threw this whale, with so many
tuns of oil in his belly, ashore at Windsor?
MISTRESS FORD, to Mistress Page, complaining
about Falstaff, *The Merry Wives of Windsor*, II, i

His humour is lofty, his discourse peremptory, his tongue filed, his eye ambitious, his gait majestical, and his general behaviour vain, ridiculous, and thrasonical. He is too picked, too spruce, too affected, too odd, as it were, too peregrinate, as I may call it.

HOLOFERNES, to Sir Nathaniel, on Armado,
Love's Labour's Lost, V, i

Unbidden guests
Are often welcomest when they are gone.
  DUKE OF BEDFORD, *King Henry the Sixth, Part I*, II, ii

> *Bedford was not in fact uttering this as an insult but*
> *rather as a reason not to accompany Talbot on a visit*
> *to the Countess of Auvergne.*

Consumption of the Purse: Poverty and Riches

MONEY, or its lack, can always rouse emotions and opinions. Although not generally the central theme in Shakespeare's work, except when it walks hand in hand with power, there are a number of references to it – from the common-sense attitude of characters like Nerissa to the greed of Philip the Bastard, to the ruefulness of Falstaff and compassion of the poor, mad King Lear.

They are as sick that surfeit with too much as they that starve with nothing. It is no mean happiness therefore, to be seated in the mean: superfluity comes sooner by white hairs, but competency lives longer.

NERISSA, to Portia, *The Merchant of Venice*, I, ii

I am not in the giving vein today.

    RICHARD III, to Buckingham, *King Richard III*, IV, ii

The Duke of Buckingham has reminded the King of his promise to give him the earldom of Hereford and assets that go with it.

Remuneration! O! that's the Latin word for three farthings.

    COSTARD, *Love's Labour's Lost*, III, i

Nothing comes amiss, so money comes withal.

    GRUMIO, *The Taming of the Shrew*, I, ii

I can get no remedy against this consumption of the purse: borrowing only lingers and lingers it out, but the disease is incurable.

    FALSTAFF, *King Henry IV, Part 2*, I, ii

He that wants money, means, and content, is without three good friends.

    CORIN, *As You Like It*, III, ii

Sell when you can, you are not for all markets.

    ROSALIND, *As You Like It*, III, v

'Tis gold
Which buys admittance; oft it doth; yea, and makes
Diana's rangers false themselves, yield up
Their deer to the stand o' the stealer; and 'tis gold
Which makes the true man kill'd and saves the thief;
Nay, sometime hangs both thief and true man: what
Can it not do and undo?

Cloten, Cymbeline, II, iii

How quickly nature falls into revolt
When gold becomes her object!

Henry IV, King Henry IV, Part 2, IV, v

Bell, book, and candle shall not drive me back,
When gold and silver becks me to come on.

Bastard, to Elinor, King John, III, ii

Seven hundred pounds and possibilities is goot gifts.

Sir Hugh Evans, The Merry Wives of Windsor, I, i

Saint-seducing gold.

Romeo, Romeo and Juliet, I, i

Neither a borrower, nor a lender be;
For loan oft loses both itself and friend.

POLONIUS, to Laertes, Hamlet, I, iii

How apt the poor are to be proud.

OLIVIA, Twelfth Night, III, i

Believe't, that we'll do anything for gold.
　　　　PHRYNIA and TIMANDRA, *Timon of Athens*, IV, iii

Far from being proud, they are referred to as 'a brace of harlots'.

O, what a world of vile ill-favour'd faults
Looks handsome in three hundred pounds a year!
　　　　MISTRESS PAGE, *The Merry Wives of Windsor*, III, iv

The poor King Reignier, whose large style
Agrees not with the leanness of his purse.
　　　　GLOUCESTER, *King Henry VI, Part 2*, I, i

Those that much covet are with gain so fond
That what they have not, that which they possess
They scatter and unloose it from their bond,
And so by hoping more they have but less.
　　　　The Rape of Lucrece

For herein Fortune shows herself more kind
Than is her custom: it is still her use
To let the wretched man outlive his wealth,
To view with hollow eye and wrinkled brow
An age of poverty.
　　　　ANTONIO, *The Merchant of Venice*, IV, i

I am as poor as Job, my lord, but not so patient.
FALSTAFF, to the Lord Chief Justice,
King Henry IV, Part 2, I, ii

Poor naked wretches, wheresoe'er you are,
That bide the pelting of this pitiless storm,
How shall your houseless heads and unfed sides,
Your loop'd and window'd raggedness, defend you
From seasons such as these? O, I have ta'en
Too little care of this! Take physic, pomp;
Expose thyself to feel what wretches feel,
That thou mayst shake the superflux to them,
And show the heavens more just.
LEAR, *King Lear*, III, iv

Evermore thanks, the exchequer of the poor.
HENRY BOLINGBROKE, to Lords Ross and Willoughby,
King Richard II, II, iii

Rich men deal gifts,
Expecting in return twenty for one?
TIMON, to Flavius, his loyal steward,
Timon of Athens, IV, iii

He is well paid that is well satisfied.
PORTIA, *The Merchant of Venice*, IV, i

FORD: If money go before, all ways do lie open.
FALSTAFF: Money is a good soldier, sir, and will on.

The Merry Wives of Windsor, II, ii

APOTHECARY: My poverty, but not my will, consents.
ROMEO: I pay thy poverty, and not thy will.

Romeo and Juliet, V, i

*Romeo has sought out the poorest apothecary in Venice,
guessing correctly that, offered plenty of money, someone
desperately poor would agree to sell him a powerful poison.*

That the gods sent not
Corn for the rich men only.

>MARCIUS, reporting the citizens' complaints
to Menenius, *Coriolanus*, I, i

This yellow slave
Will knit and break religions, bless the accursed,
Make the hoar leprosy adored, place thieves
And give them title, knee and approbation
With senators on the bench.

>TIMON, *Timon of Athens*, IV, iii

The 'yellow slave' is, of course, gold.

Whiles I am a beggar, I will rail
And say there is no sin but to be rich;
And being rich, my virtue then shall be
To say there is no vice but beggary.

>BASTARD, *King John*, II, i

LORD CHIEF JUSTICE: Your means are very slender, and your
waste is great.
FALSTAFF: I would it were otherwise; I would my means
were greater, and my waist slenderer.

>*King Henry IV, Part 2*, I, ii

Strange Capers: Men, Women, Love and Marriage

How Shakespeare's men see themselves, how they see women – how his women see themselves, and how they see men. Although not all of the quotations in this section concern the relationship between men and women, a large number of them do, given that that relationship forms the linchpin of many of the comedies – not to forget the most famous love story of all, *Romeo and Juliet* – or, if not central to the play, the relationship is, perhaps, essential to a sub-plot.

Roses have thorns, and silver fountains mud;
Clouds and eclipses stain both moon and sun,
And loathsome canker lives in sweetest bud.
All men make faults.

SONNET XXXV

As, apparently, everybody seems to turn against him,
man does not delight Lear either:

Blow, winds, and crack your cheeks! rage! blow!
You cataracts and hurricanoes, spout
Till you have drench'd our steeples, drown'd the cocks!
You sulphurous and thought-executing fires,
Vaunt-couriers to oak-cleaving thunderbolts,
Singe my white head! And thou, all-shaking thunder,
Strike flat the thick rotundity o' the world!
Crack nature's moulds, all germens spill at once
That make ingrateful man!

LEAR, *King Lear*, III, ii

A theme which is dealt with much more lightly in a song
in one of the comedies:

Blow, blow, thou winter wind.
Thou art not so unkind
As man's ingratitude.

AMIENS, *As You Like It*, II, vii

What a piece of work is a man! how noble in reason! how infinite in faculty! in form and moving how express and admirable! in action how like an angel! in apprehension how like a god! the beauty of the world! the paragon of animals!

HAMLET, to Rosencrantz and Guildenstern,
Hamlet, II, ii

He finishes up, 'Man delights not me: no, nor woman neither,' but seems here to mean mankind in general.

Lord, what fools these mortals be!

PUCK, *A Midsummer Night's Dream*, III, ii

If you prick us, do we not bleed? if you tickle us, do we
not laugh? if you poison us, do we not die? And if you
wrong us, shall we not revenge?

SHYLOCK, *The Merchant of Venice*, III, i

*Shylock's impassioned – and witty – argument is a defence of
Jews, but could in fact apply to any individual or any group who
feel that they are not being treated as they deserve.*

On Men

Give me leave
To tell you once again that at my birth
The front of heaven was full of fiery shapes,
The goats ran from the mountains, and the herds
Were strangely clamorous to the frighted fields.
These signs have mark'd me extraordinary;
And all the courses of my life do show
I am not in the roll of common men.

GLENDOWER, *King Henry IV, Part 1*, III, i

*This vainglorious bombast continues, to be brought short –
temporarily – by Hotspur's brief response: 'I think there's no man
speaks better Welsh. I'll to dinner.'*

'Tis ever common
That men are merriest when they are from home.

HENRY V, *King Henry V*, I, ii

His life was gentle, and the elements
So mix'd in him that Nature might stand up
And say to all the world 'This was a man!'

MARK ANTONY, of Brutus, *Julius Caesar*, V, v

A kind heart he hath: a woman would run through fire
and water for such a kind heart.

MISTRESS QUICKLY, of Fenton,
The Merry Wives of Windsor, III, iv

'Tis not a year or two shows us a man:
They are all but stomachs, and we all but food;
To eat us hungerly, and when they are full,
They belch us.

EMILIA, to Desdemona, *Othello*, III, iv

Men's vows are women's traitors!

IMOGEN, *Cymbeline*, III, iv

We'll have a swashing and a martial outside,
As many other mannish cowards have.

ROSALIND, *As You Like It*, IV, ii

Planning her disguise as a man.

There's no trust,
No faith, no honesty in men; all perjured,
All forsworn, all naught, all dissemblers.
NURSE, Romeo and Juliet, III, ii

I see a man's life is a tedious one.

IMOGEN, *Cymbeline*, III, vi

Imogen is disguised as a page, calling herself 'Fidele'.

Would it not grieve a woman to be overmastered with a piece of valiant dust? to make an account of her life to a clod of wayward marl?

BEATRICE, *Much Ado About Nothing*, II, i

On Women

How hard it is for women to keep counsel!

PORTIA, *Julius Caesar*, II, iv

Certainly a woman's thought runs before her actions.

ROSALIND (disguised as a youth), to Orlando,
As You Like It, IV, i

Come on, come on; you are pictures out of doors,
Bells in your parlours, wild-cats in your kitchens,
Saints in your injuries, devils being offended,
Players in your housewifery, and housewives in your beds.

IAGO, to Emilia and Desdemona, *Othello*, II, i

Or else she could not have the wit to do this: the wiser,
the waywarder: make the doors upon a woman's wit and it
will out at the casement; shut that and 'twill out at the
key-hole; stop that, 'twill fly with the smoke out at the
chimney.

ROSALIND (disguised as a youth), to Orlando,
As You Like It, IV, i

I have no other, but a woman's reason;
I think him so because I think him so.

LUCETTA, The Two Gentlemen of Verona, I, ii

She explains to Julia why she thinks Proteus the best of Julia's
suitors.

Rich she shall be, that's certain; wise, or I'll none;
virtuous, or I'll never cheapen her; fair, or I'll never look
on her; mild, or come not near me; noble, or not I for an
angel; of good discourse, an excellent musician, and her
hair shall be of what colour it please God.

BENEDICK, Much Ado About Nothing, II, iii

Having witnessed his friend Claudio's behaviour on falling in
love, Benedick is most scornful. He wouldn't behave like that – he
wouldn't even contemplate a woman who didn't have the
qualities he lists; there is something rather engaging in his not
being fussy about hair colour – very kindly leaving that to God.

Do you not know I am a woman? when I think, I must speak.

Rosalind (in her disguise), to Celia,
As You Like It, III, ii

There was never yet fair woman but she made mouths in a glass.

Fool, *King Lear*, III, ii

When a world of men
Could not prevail with all their oratory,
Yet hath a woman's kindness over-ruled.

Talbot, to Bedford and Burgundy,
Henry VI, Part 1, II, ii

On Love

Love is a smoke raised with the fume of sighs;
Being purged, a fire sparkling in lovers' eyes;
Being vex'd, a sea nourish'd with lovers' tears:
What is it else? a madness most discreet,
A choking gall and a preserving sweet.

Romeo, *Romeo and Juliet*, I, i

And he hasn't even met her yet . . .

Love is a spirit all compact of fire,
Not gross to sink, but light, and will aspire.

Venus and Adonis

We that are true lovers run into strange capers; but as all is mortal in nature, so is all nature in love mortal in folly.

Touchstone, *As You Like It*, II, iv

Cleopatra: If it be love indeed, tell me how much.
Antony: There's beggary in the love that can be reckon'd.

Antony and Cleopatra, I, i

VALENTINE: Why, how know you that I am in love?

SPEED: Marry, by these special marks: first, you have learned, like Sir Proteus, to wreathe your arms, like a malcontent; to relish a love-song, like a robin-redbreast; to walk alone, like one that had the pestilence; to sigh, like a schoolboy that had lost his A B C; to weep, like a young wench that had buried her grandam; to fast, like one that takes diet; to watch like one that fears robbing; to speak puling, like a beggar at Hallowmas. You were wont, when you laughed, to crow like a cock; when you walked, to walk like one of the lions; when you fasted, it was presently after dinner; when you looked sadly, it was for want of money: and now you are metamorphosed with a mistress, that, when I look on you, I can hardly think you my master.

The Two Gentlemen of Verona, II, i

Doubt thou the stars are fire;
Doubt that the sun doth move;
Doubt truth to be a liar;
But never doubt I love.

HAMLET, *Hamlet*, II, ii

In a letter to Ophelia, read out by Polonius.

I do much wonder that one man, seeing how much another man is a fool when he dedicates his behaviours to love, will, after he hath laughed at such shallow follies in others, become the argument of his own scorn by falling in love.

BENEDICK, on Claudio, *Much Ado About Nothing*, II, iii

Cupid is a knavish lad,
Thus to make poor females mad.
                    PUCK, *A Midsummer Night's Dream*, III, ii

When my love swears that she is made of truth,
I do believe her, though I know she lies.
                                        SONNET CXXXVIII

This whimpled, whining, purblind, wayward boy;
This senior-junior, giant-dwarf, Dan Cupid;
Regent of love-rhymes, lord of folded arms,
The anointed sovereign of sighs and groans,
Liege of all loiterers and malcontents,
Dread prince of plackets, king of codpieces . . .
                    BEROWNE, *Love's Labour's Lost*, III, i

I will attend her here,
And woo her with some spirit when she comes.
Say that she rail; why then I'll tell her plain
She sings as sweetly as a nightingale:
Say that she frown, I'll say she looks as clear
As morning roses newly wash'd with dew:
Say she be mute and will not speak a word;
Then I'll commend her volubility,
And say she uttereth piercing eloquence:
If she do bid me pack, I'll give her thanks,
As though she bid me stay by her a week:
If she deny to wed, I'll crave the day
When I shall ask the banns and when be married.

PETRUCHIO, *The Taming of the Shrew*, II, i

If thou remember'st not the slightest folly
That ever love did make thee run into,
Thou hast not loved.

SILVIUS, to Corin, *As You Like It*, II, iv

There lives within the very flame of love
A kind of wick or snuff that will abate it.

CLAUDIUS, to Laertes, *Hamlet*, IV, vii

By heaven, I do love: and it hath taught me to rhyme and
to be melancholy; and here is part of my rhyme, and here
my melancholy.

BEROWNE, *Love's Labour's Lost*, IV, iii

I had rather hear my dog bark at a crow than a man swear
he loves me.

BEATRICE, to Benedick,
Much Ado About Nothing, I, i

My mistress' eyes are nothing like the sun;
Coral is far more red than her lips' red:
If snow be white, why then her breasts are dun;
If hairs be wires, black wires grow on her head.

SONNET CXXX

Love is not love
Which alters when it alteration finds,
Or bends with the remover to remove:
O no! it is an ever-fixed mark
That looks on tempests and is never shaken;
It is the star to every wandering bark,
Whose worth's unknown, although his height be taken.

SONNET CXVI

For I cannot be
Mine own, nor any thing to any, if
I be not thine.

FLORIZEL, to Perdita, *The Winter's Tale*, IV, iv

*Prince Florizel believes that Perdita is just a simple
shepherdess.*

I loved Ophelia: forty thousand brothers
Could not, with all their quantity of love,
Make up my sum. What wilt thou do for her? . . .
. . . 'Swounds, show me what thou'lt do:
Woo't weep? woo't fight? woo't fast? woo't tear thyself?
Woo't drink up eisel? eat a crocodile?
I'll do't. Dost thou come here to whine?
To outface me with leaping in her grave?
Be buried quick with her, and so will I:
And, if thou prate of mountains, let them throw
Millions of acres on us, till our ground,
Singeing his pate against the burning zone,
Make Ossa like a wart! Nay, an thou'lt mouth,
I'll rant as well as thou.

HAMLET, *Hamlet*, V, i

At the graveyard. Hamlet, shocked by learning that Ophelia is
dead, is infuriated that Laertes should have the effrontery to
display a grief that he feels comes nowhere near to his own.
He seems more overcome by what he sees as a slight than
by distress at Ophelia's death.

No, faith, die by attorney. The poor world is almost six thousand years old, and in all this time there was not any man died in his own person, videlicit, in a love-cause ... men have died from time to time and worms have eaten them, but not for love.

ROSALIND, *As You Like It*, IV, i

A douche of common sense from Rosalind (disguised), who has just elicited from Orlando the assertion that he would die if Rosalind wouldn't have him.

For I cannot be
Mine own, nor any thing to any, if
I be not thine.

FLORIZEL, to Perdita, *The Winter's Tale*, IV, iv

Prince Florizel believes that Perdita is just a simple shepherdess.

On Marriage

For what is wedlock forced, but a hell,
An age of discord and continual strife?
Whereas the contrary bringeth bliss,
And is a pattern of celestial peace.

EARL OF SUFFOLK, *King Henry VI, Part 1*, V, v

Hasty marriage seldom proveth well.
> RICHARD PLANTAGENET, Duke of Gloucester,
> *King Henry VI, Part 3*, IV, i

He is the half part of a blessed man,
Left to be finished by such as she;
And she a fair divided excellence,
Whose fulness of perfection lies in him.
O, two such silver currents, when they join,
Do glorify the banks that bound them in.
> FIRST CITIZEN, *King John*, II, i

I could not endure a husband with a beard on his face:
I had rather lie in the woollen.
> BEATRICE, *Much Ado About Nothing*, II, i

When I said I would die a bachelor, I did not think I
should live till I were married.
> BENEDICK, *Much Ado About Nothing*, II, iii

A young man married is a man that's marred.
> PAROLLES, *All's Well That Ends Well*, II, iii

*'A very tainted fellow, and full of wickedness', Parolles uses
these words to persuade Bertram to leave his new wife and seek
a life of vice.*

I will be master of what is mine own:
She is my goods, my chattels; she is my house,
My household stuff, my field, my barn,
My horse, my ox, my ass, my any thing;
And here she stands, touch her whoever dare.

PETRUCHIO, *The Taming of the Shrew*, III, ii

*This view of the relationship between men and women in
Elizabethan England is perhaps not wrong, although
exaggerated, but certainly not true of most of Shakespeare's
heroines, who show quite a bit more spirit than chattels . . .
Petruchio hauls Katharina off at this stage, leaving their friends
to pronounce a much more modern-sounding verdict: Gremio:
'Went they not quickly, I should die with laughing.' Tranio: 'Of
all mad matches never was the like.' Lucentio: 'Mistress, what's
your opinion of your sister?' Bianca: 'That, being mad herself,
she's madly mated'. Gremio: 'I warrant him, Petruchio is Kated.'*

Let husbands know
Their wives have sense like them: they see and smell
And have their palates both for sweet and sour,
As husbands have . . . have not we affections,
Desires for sport, and frailty, as men have?
Then let them use us well: else let them know,
The ills we do, their ills instruct us so.

EMILIA, to Desdemona, *Othello*, IV, iii

*Emilia, Iago's wife, speaks up for women in terms
very similar to those of Shylock's famous speech.*

Fools are as like husbands as pilchards are to herrings; the husband's the bigger.

FESTE, the Clown, to Viola, *Twelfth Night*, III, i

Get thee a good husband, and use him as he uses thee.

PAROLLES, *All's Well That Ends Well*, I, i

I have been, madam, a wicked creature, as you and all flesh and blood are; and, indeed, I do marry that I may repent.

CLOWN, *All's Well That Ends Well*, I, iii

Men are April when they woo, December when they wed: maids are May when they are maids, but the sky changes when they are wives.

ROSALIND (in her disguise), to Orlando,
As You Like It, IV, i

If men could be contented to be what they are, there were no fear in marriage.

CLOWN, *All's Well That Ends Well*, I, iii

Many a good hanging prevents a bad marriage.

FESTE, the Clown, *Twelfth Night*, I, v

Wise Enough
to Play the Fool:
Fools, Clowns
and Comic Relief

This fellow is wise enough to play the fool;
And to do that well craves a kind of wit:
He must observe their mood on whom he jests,
The quality of persons, and the time,
And, like the haggard, check at every feather
That comes before his eye. This is a practice
As full of labour as a wise man's art:
For folly that he wisely shows is fit;
But wise men, folly-fall'n, quite taint their wit.

VIOLA, *Twelfth Night*, III, i

S HAKESPEARE often included a fool in his plays – the
character is frequently a professional jester (these were
employed at court or by the nobility in Shakespeare's day),
and usually a boldly witty and acute comedian. Although
sometimes – as with Feste in *Twelfth Night* – called 'Clown',

Shakespeare also used another kind of clown in his drama. This clown is usually a good and innocent character; ignorant, sometimes dull-witted, who on many occasions blunders into a situation quite outside his scope. Some of the clowns are, like the fools, definite characters who appear on and off throughout the plays – like Dogberry in *Much Ado About Nothing* or Costard in *Love's Labour's Lost*. Other are incidental, appearing only once or twice in the role of, say, porter or shepherd; some of these are sharp-tongued enough to be 'fools' – the servant in *Troilus and Cressida*, for instance. In comedies, their role is to keep the comic action going, maybe as a kind of side-show; in tragedies, they provide relief from the tension and serve to make the action that follows more hard-hitting.

The comedy is usually in the form of interaction, generally dialogue, between a fool or clown and a 'straight' character, but can be between two straight characters or two clowns. In *Hamlet*, Hamlet – who is a prince, and must therefore, to his face at least, be treated with respect, whatever he does or says – comic dialogue comes in the form of his teasing of Polonius and Osric under the cover of feigned madness.

SECOND MURDERER: What, shall we stab him as he sleeps?
FIRST MURDERER: No; then he will say 'twas done cowardly, when he wakes.

King Richard III, I, iv

The Duke of Gloucester has sent them to kill his imprisoned brother, the Duke of Clarence.

Speed, Valentine's page, cannot find his master, who he thinks might have left for Milan. Proteus, Valentine's friend, has entrusted Speed with a letter to Julia, with whom he is infatuated.

SPEED: Twenty to one then he is shipp'd already,
And I have play'd the sheep in losing him.
PROTEUS: Indeed, a sheep doth very often stray,
An if the shepherd be a while away.
SPEED: You conclude that my master is a shepherd, then,
and I a sheep?
PROTEUS: I do.
SPEED: Why then, my horns are his horns, whether I wake
or sleep.
PROTEUS: A silly answer and fitting well a sheep.
SPEED: This proves me still a sheep.
PROTEUS: True; and thy master a shepherd.
SPEED: Nay, that I can deny by a circumstance.
PROTEUS: It shall go hard but I'll prove it by another.
SPEED: The shepherd seeks the sheep, and not the sheep the
shepherd; but I seek my master, and my master seeks not
me: therefore I am no sheep.
PROTEUS: The sheep for fodder follow the shepherd; the
shepherd for food follows not the sheep: thou for wages
followest thy master; thy master for wages
follows not thee: therefore thou art a sheep.
SPEED: Such another proof will make me cry 'baa'.
PROTEUS: But, dost thou hear? gavest thou my letter to Julia?
SPEED: Ay sir: I, a lost mutton, gave your letter to her, a laced
mutton, and she, a laced mutton, gave me, a lost mutton,
nothing for my labour.
PROTEUS: Here's too small a pasture for such store of
muttons.

The Two Gentlemen of Verona, I, i

The clowns in Hamlet *are grave-diggers who, in providing some comic relief, also present a much simpler and more accepting view of death than those brooded over by Hamlet.*

HAMLET: Whose grave's this, sirrah?

FIRST CLOWN: Mine, sir

HAMLET: I think it be thine, indeed; for thou liest in't.

FIRST CLOWN: You lie out on't, sir, and therefore it is not yours: for my part, I do not lie in't, and yet it is mine.

HAMLET: Thou dost lie in't, to be in't and say it is thine: 'tis for the dead, not for the quick; therefore thou liest.

FIRST CLOWN: 'Tis a quick lie, sir; 'twill away gain, from me to you.

HAMLET: What man dost thou dig it for?

FIRST CLOWN: For no man, sir.

HAMLET: What woman, then?

FIRST CLOWN: For none, neither.

HAMLET: Who is to be buried in't?

FIRST CLOWN: One that was a woman, sir; but, rest her soul, she's dead . . .

Hamlet asks the clown how long he has been a gravedigger.

FIRST CLOWN: . . . the very day that young Hamlet was born; he that is mad, and sent into England.

HAMLET: Ay, marry, why was he sent into England?

FIRST CLOWN: Why, because he was mad: he shall recover his wits there; or, if he do not, it's no great matter there.

HAMLET: Why?

FIRST CLOWN: 'Twill not be seen in him there; there the men are as mad as he.

HAMLET: How came he mad?

FIRST CLOWN: Very strangely, they say.

HAMLET: How strangely?

FIRST CLOWN: Faith, e'en with losing his wits.

HAMLET: Upon what ground?
FIRST CLOWN: Why, here in Denmark.

Hamlet, V, i

Dogberry, the constable, instructs the watchmen:

If you meet a thief, you may suspect him, by virtue of your office, to be no true man; and, for such kind of men, the less you meddle or make with them, why the more is for your honesty.
WATCHMAN: If we know him to be a thief, shall we not lay hands on him?
DOGBERRY: Truly, by your office, you may; but I think they that touch pitch will be defiled: the most peaceable way for you, if you do take a thief, is to let him show himself what he is and steal out of your company.

Much Ado About Nothing, III, iii

BEROWNE: Good my knave,
   Do one thing for me that I shall entreat.
COSTARD: When would you have it done, sir?
BEROWNE : This afternoon.
COSTARD : Well, I will do it, sir: fare you well.
BEROWNE : Thou knowest not what it is.
COSTARD : I shall know, sir, when I have done it.

Love's Labour's Lost, III, i

A tableau, The Nine Worthies, *is to be performed.*

COSTARD: Sir, they would know
    Whether the three Worthies shall come in or no.
BEROWNE: What, are there but three?
COSTARD: No, sir; but it is vara fine,
    For every one pursents three.
BEROWNE: And three times thrice is nine.
COSTARD:
    Not so, sir; under correction, sir; I hope it is not so.
    You cannot beg us, sir, I can assure you, sir we know what
    we know: I hope, sir, three times thrice, sir, –
BEROWNE: Is not nine.
COSTARD: Under correction, sir, we know whereuntil it doth
    amount.
BEROWNE: By Jove, I always took three threes for nine.
COSTARD: O Lord, sir, it were pity you should get your living
    by reckoning, sir.
BEROWNE: How much is it?
COSTARD: O Lord, sir, the parties themselves, the actors, sir,
    will show whereuntil it doth amount: for mine own part, I
    am, as they say, but to parfect one man in one poor man,
    Pompion the Great, sir.
BEROWNE: Art thou one of the Worthies?
COSTARD: It pleased them to think me worthy of Pompion
    the Great: for mine own part, I know not the degree of
    the Worthy, but I am to stand for him.

Love's Labour's Lost, V, ii

Costard proceeds to get muddled and in the actual presentation at
court announces himself as 'Pompey the Big'.

Autolycus, the knavish thief, 'a snapper-up of unconsidered
trifles', meets the Shepherd and his son, the Clown, on their way
to prove to Polixenes that Perdita is not the Shepherd's daughter.
Autolycus and Florizel have exchanged clothing.

SHEPHERD: My business, sir, is to the king.
AUTOLYCUS: What advocate hast thou to him?
SHEPHERD: I know not, an't like you.
CLOWN: Advocate's the court-word for a pheasant: say you
  have none.
SHEPHERD: None, sir; I have no pheasant, cock nor hen.
AUTOLYCUS: How blessed are we that are not simple men!
  Yet nature might have made me as these are,
  Therefore I will not disdain.
CLOWN: This cannot be but a great courtier.
SHEPHERD: His garments are rich, but he wears them not
  handsomely.
CLOWN: He seems to be the more noble in being fantastical:
  a great man, I'll warrant; I know by the picking on's teeth.
                                    The Winter's Tale, IV, iv

TOUCHSTONE: Wast ever in court, shepherd?
CORIN: No, truly.
TOUCHSTONE: Then thou art damned.
CORIN: Nay, I hope.
TOUCHSTONE: Truly, thou art damned like an ill-roasted egg,
  all on one side.
CORIN: For not being at court? Your reason.
TOUCHSTONE: Why, if thou never wast at court, thou never
  sawest good manners; if thou never sawest good manners,
  then thy manners must be wicked; and wickedness is sin,
  and sin is damnation. Thou art in a parlous state, shepherd.
                          TOUCHSTONE, *As You Like It*, III, ii

Olivia: Take the fool away.

Clown (Feste): Do you not hear, fellows? Take away the lady.

Olivia: Go to, you're a dry fool; I'll no more of you: besides, you grow dishonest.

Clown: Two faults, madonna, that drink and good counsel will amend: for give the dry fool drink, then is the fool not dry: bid the dishonest man mend himself; if he mend, he is no longer dishonest; if he cannot, let the botcher mend him. Any thing that's mended is but patched: virtue that transgresses is but patched with sin; and sin that amends is but patched with virtue. If that this simple syllogism will serve, so; if it will not, what remedy? As there is no true cuckold but calamity, so beauty's a flower. The lady bade take away the fool; therefore, I say again, take her away.

Twelfth Night, I, v

The dullness of the fool is the whetstone of the wits.

Celia, *As You Like It*, I, ii

*King Lear, who has already disinherited Cordelia, has now
quarrelled with his daughter Goneril, and is preparing to go to
his other daughter, Regan. The Fool can see better than him
how things stand . . .*

FOOL: Thou canst tell why one's nose stands i' the middle
　　on's face?

LEAR: No.

FOOL: Why, to keep one's eyes of either side's nose; that what
　　a man cannot smell out, he may spy into.

LEAR: I did her wrong –

FOOL: Canst tell how an oyster makes his shell?

LEAR: No.

FOOL: Nor I neither; but I can tell why a snail has a house.

LEAR: Why?

FOOL: Why, to put his head in; not to give it away to his
　　daughters, and leave his horns without a case.

LEAR: . . . Be my horses ready?

FOOL: Thy asses are gone about 'em. The reason why the
　　seven stars are no more than seven is a pretty reason.

LEAR: Because they are not eight?

FOOL: Yes, indeed: thou wouldst make a good fool.

LEAR: To take 't again perforce! Monster ingratitude!

FOOL: If thou wert my fool, nuncle, I'd have thee beaten for
　　being old before thy time.

LEAR: How's that?

FOOL: Thou shouldst not have been old till thou hadst been
　　wise.

King Lear, I, v

*Cleopatra has sent for 'a rural fellow', who arrives bearing
a basket of figs for her.*

CLEOPATRA: Hast thou the pretty worm of Nilus there,
That kills and pains not?

CLOWN: Truly, I have him: but I would not be the party that
should desire you to touch him, for his biting is immortal;
those that do die of it do seldom or never recover.

CLEOPATRA: Rememberest thou any that have died on't?

CLOWN: Very many, men and women too. I heard of one of
them no longer than yesterday: a very honest woman, but
something given to lie; as a woman should not do, but in
the way of honesty: how she died of the biting of it, what
pain she felt: truly, she makes a very good report o' the
worm; but he that will believe all that they say, shall never
be saved by half that they do: but this is most fallible, the
worm's an odd worm.

Antony and Cleopatra, V, ii

FIRST CITIZEN: . . .the many-headed multitude.

THIRD CITIZEN: We have been called so of many; not that
our heads are some brown, some black, some auburn,
some bald, but that our wits are so diversely coloured: and
truly I think if all our wits were to issue out of one skull,
they would fly east, west, north, south, and their consent
of one direct way should be at once to all the points o' the
compass.

SECOND CITIZEN: Think you so? Which way do you judge
my wit would fly?

THIRD CITIZEN: Nay, your wit will not so soon out as
another man's will; 'tis strongly wedged up in a block-
head, but if it were at liberty, 'twould, sure, southward.

[143]

SECOND CITIZEN: Why that way?

THIRD CITIZEN: To lose itself in a fog, where being three parts melted away with rotten dews, the fourth would return for conscience sake, to help to get thee a wife.

SECOND CITIZEN: You are never without your tricks: you may, you may.

THIRD CITIZEN: Are you all resolved to give your voices? But that's no matter, the greater part carries it. I say, if he would incline to the people, there was never a worthier man.

Coriolanus, II, iii

Hamlet has put on an 'antic disposition', pretending madness but, as he tells Rosencrantz and Guildenstern, he is 'but mad north-north-west: when the wind is southerly I know a hawk from a handsaw', a particularly witty expression as a hawk is not just the bird of prey but also, like a handsaw, a tool (used by plasterers); however, 'handsaw' sounds like 'heronsew', an archaic word for another bird – a small or young heron. Here poor pompous Polonius is teased into making a fool of himself.

HAMLET: Do you see yonder cloud that's almost in shape of a camel?

POLONIUS: By the mass, and 'tis like a camel, indeed.

HAMLET: Methinks it is like a weasel.

POLONIUS: It is backed like a weasel.

HAMLET: Or like a whale?

POLONIUS: Very like a whale.

Hamlet, III, ii

CITIZENS: Faith, we hear fearful news.
FIRST CITIZEN: For mine own part,
   When I said, banish him, I said 'twas pity.
SECOND CITIZEN: And so did I.
THIRD CITIZEN: And so did I; and, to say the truth, so did
   very many of us: that we did, we did for the best; and
   though we willingly consented to his banishment, yet it
   was against our will.

Coriolanus, IV, iv

*Irritated by Pandarus's impertinent questioning, Paris's servant
pretends to misunderstand him.*

PANDARUS: Friend, you! pray you, a word: do not you follow
   the young Lord Paris?
SERVANT: Ay, sir, when he goes before me.
PANDARUS: You depend upon him, I mean?
SERVANT: Sir, I do depend upon the lord.
PANDARUS: You depend upon a noble gentleman; I must
   needs praise him.
SERVANT: The lord be praised!
PANDARUS: You know me, do you not?
SERVANT: Faith, sir, superficially.
PANDARUS: Friend, know me better; I am the Lord Pandarus.
SERVANT: I hope I shall know your honour better.
PANDARUS: I do desire it.
SERVANT: You are in the state of grace.
PANDARUS: Grace! not so, friend: honour and lordship are
   my titles. [*Music within*] What music is this?
SERVANT: I do but partly know, sir: it is music in parts.
PANDARUS: Know you the musicians?
SERVANT: Wholly, sir.

PANDARUS: Who play they to?

SERVANT: To the hearers, sir.

PANDARUS: At whose pleasure, friend?

SERVANT: At mine, sir, and theirs that love music.

PANDARUS: Command, I mean, friend.

SERVANT: Who shall I command, sir?

PANDARUS: Friend, we understand not one another: I am too courtly and thou art too cunning. At whose request do these men play?

SERVANT: That's to 't indeed, sir: marry, sir, at the request of Paris my lord, who's there in person.

Troilus and Cressida, III, i

MACDUFF: I believe drink gave thee the lie last night.

PORTER: That it did, sir, i' the very throat on me: but I requited him for his lie; and, I think, being too strong for him, though he took up my legs sometime, yet I made a shift to cast him.

Macbeth, II, iii

*Foppish Osric arrives, flourishing his extravagant hat, with a
message for Hamlet, who decides to have a bit of fun.*

HAMLET: Put your bonnet to his right use; 'tis for the head.
OSRIC: I thank your lordship, it is very hot.
HAMLET: No, believe me, 'tis very cold; the wind is northerly.
OSRIC: It is indifferent cold, my lord, indeed.
HAMLET: But yet methinks it is very sultry and hot for my
    complexion.
OSRIC: Exceedingly, my lord; it is very sultry, – as 'twere, – I
    cannot tell how.

Hamlet, V, ii

Wit, an't be thy will, put me into good fooling!
Those wits, that think they have thee, do very oft
prove fools; and I, that am sure I lack thee, may
pass for a wise man: for what says Quinapalus?
'Better a witty fool, than a foolish wit.'

FESTE, the Clown, *Twelfth Night*, I, v

Feste, addressing Wit, quotes an invented ancient philosopher.

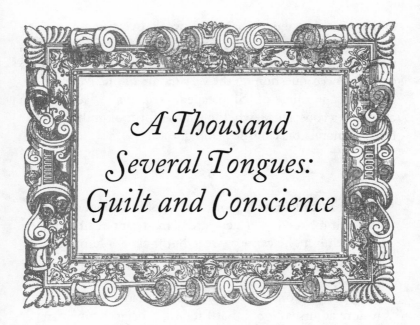

A Thousand Several Tongues: Guilt and Conscience

THE AWARENESS of right and wrong haunts Shakespeare's works – with the recognition that black is not always all black and white all white. The word 'conscience' crops up time and again in the plays, its meaning ranging from a simple declaration of solemnity – 'upon my conscience' – to the far more complex one of moral knowledge (it is, after all, from the Latin *conscientia*, meaning knowledge or consciousness), awareness or insight. From this is derived the usual modern definition of 'conscience' – the sense of what is right and what is wrong, and of guilt when one commits an action one knows to be wrong. This is the kind of conscience the Second Murderer and Launcelot Gobbo have to grapple with in the quotations below: for them their conscience speaks before they act – a kind of moral master. For others it comes in the form of guilt and remorse, as, too late, the likes of Lady Macbeth and Richard III realize the enormity of their crimes and their consciences begin to work overtime. Hamlet's conscience is at once more subtle and more wide-ranging, roaming over the pros and cons of every action and its consequences, questioning the very nature of life. Many of the greatest speeches of Shakespeare's plays arise from a character's conscience, whether in the form of guilt or in the form of moral consciousness and questing.

I'll not meddle with it [conscience]: it is a dangerous thing: it makes a man a coward: a man cannot steal, but it accuseth him; he cannot swear, but it checks him; he cannot lie with his neighbour's wife, but it detects him: 'tis a blushing shamefast spirit that mutinies in a man's bosom; it fills one full of obstacles: it made me once restore a purse of gold that I found; it beggars any man that keeps it: it is turned out of all towns and cities for a dangerous thing; and every man that means to live well endeavours to trust to himself and to live without it.

SECOND MURDERER, *Richard III*, I, iv

Every man's conscience is a thousand swords,
To fight against that bloody homicide.

OXFORD, *King Richard III*, V, ii

*The Earl of Oxford is one of the followers of the Earl
of Richmond (later Henry VII), who in due course kills
Richard III in battle.*

The fiend is at mine elbow and tempts me saying to me 'Gobbo, Launcelot Gobbo, good Launcelot', or 'good Gobbo', or 'good Launcelot Gobbo, use your legs, take the start, run away.' My conscience says 'No; take heed, honest Launcelot; take heed, honest Gobbo,' or, as aforesaid, 'honest Launcelot Gobbo; do not run; scorn running with thy heels.' Well, the most courageous fiend bids me pack: 'Via!' says the fiend; 'away!' says the fiend; 'for the heavens, rouse up a brave mind,' says the fiend, 'and run.' Well, my conscience, hanging about the neck of my heart, says very wisely to me 'My honest friend Launcelot, being an honest man's son,' or rather an honest woman's son . . . well, my conscience says 'Launcelot, budge not.' 'Budge,' says the fiend. 'Budge not,' says my conscience. 'Conscience,' say I, 'you counsel well;' ' Fiend,' say I, 'you counsel well' . . . my conscience, my conscience is but a kind of hard conscience . . . I will run.

LAUNCELOT GOBBO, *The Merchant of Venice*, II, ii

FIRST MURDERER: Remember our reward, when the deed is done.
SECOND MURDERER: 'Zounds, he dies: I had forgot the reward.
FIRST MURDERER: Where is thy conscience now?
SECOND MURDERER: In the Duke of Gloucester's purse.
FIRST MURDERER: So when he opens his purse to give us our reward, thy conscience flies out.

King Richard III, I, iv

O coward conscience, how dost thou afflict me!
The lights burn blue. It is now dead midnight.
Cold fearful drops stand on my trembling flesh.
What do I fear? myself? there's none else by:
Richard loves Richard; that is, I am I.
Is there a murderer here? No. Yes, I am.

RICHARD III, *King Richard III*, V, iii

My conscience hath a thousand several tongues,
And every tongue brings in a several tale,
And every tale condemns me for a villain.
Perjury, perjury, in the high'st degree
Murder, stern murder, in the direst degree;
All several sins, all used in each degree,
Throng to the bar, crying all, Guilty! guilty!

RICHARD III, *King Richard III*, V, iii

It takes eleven ghosts, appearing in a dream to the murderous
King, to awaken his conscience.

Conscience is but a word that cowards use,
Devised at first to keep the strong in awe:
Our strong arms be our conscience, swords our law.

RICHARD III, *King Richard III*, V, iii

Men must learn now with pity to dispense;
For policy sits above conscience.

FIRST STRANGER, *Timon of Athens*, III, ii

We know enough, if we know we are the king's subjects: if his cause be wrong, our obedience to the king wipes the crime of it out of us.

BATES, King Henry V, V, iv

The soldier rejects feelings of guilt – 'we were only following orders' – arguing that the fact that they were obeying the King expunges all culpability.

The lady protests too much, methinks.

QUEEN GERTRUDE, Hamlet, III, ii

She is commenting on the behaviour in Hamlet's play of the character who, although she hasn't realized it, represents herself.

Suspicion always haunts the guilty mind;
The thief doth fear each bush an officer.

GLOUCESTER, King Henry VI, Part 3, V, vi

How fain, like Pilate, would I wash my hands
Of this most grievous guilty murder done!

SECOND MURDERER, Richard III, I, iv

Love is too young to know what conscience is;
Yet who knows not conscience is born of love?

SONNET CLI

If it were done when 'tis done, then 'twere well
It were done quickly: if the assassination
Could trammel up the consequence, and catch
With his surcease success; that but this blow
Might be the be-all and the end-all here . . .
But in these cases
We still have judgment here . . . this even-handed justice
Commends the ingredients of our poison'd chalice
To our own lips.

MACBETH, Macbeth, I, vii

An intelligent and sensitive man, with some moral sense,
Macbeth has strong misgivings about killing Duncan, especially
– as he goes on to say – as his proposed victim is a virtuous man
and a good ruler. 'I have no spur/To prick the sides of my intent,
but only/Vaulting ambition, which o'erleaps itself/And falls on
the other.' And Lady Macbeth.

Whence is that knocking?
How is't with me, when every noise appals me?
What hands are here? ha! they pluck out mine eyes.
Will all great Neptune's ocean wash this blood
Clean from my hand? No, this my hand will rather
The multitudinous seas incarnadine,
Making the green one red.

MACBETH, Macbeth, II, ii

The moment he has committed the crime, it begins to haunt him.

Methought I heard a voice cry 'Sleep no more!
Macbeth does murder sleep', the innocent sleep,
Sleep that knits up the ravell'd sleave of care,
The death of each day's life, sore labour's bath,
Balm of hurt minds, great nature's second course,
Chief nourisher in life's feast.

MACBETH, Macbeth, II, ii

Thou canst not say I did it: never shake
Thy gory locks at me.

MACBETH, Macbeth, III, iv

*To Banquo's ghost: it is true, he did not actually do it – but he
did order Banquo killed, and he cannot escape feelings of guilt.
But he can't stop now: 'I am in blood/Stepp'd in so far that,
should I wade no more, /Returning were as tedious as go o'er'.*

*In spite of Macbeth's ramblings, it is Lady Macbeth, the prime
mover, whom guilt eventually sends mad. She walks and raves in
her sleep, remembering the words she used to spur her husband –
'a soldier, and afeard?'*

Out, damned spot! out, I say! – One: two: why, then, 'tis
time to do't. – Hell is murky! – Fie, my lord, fie! a soldier,
and afeard? What need we fear who knows it, when none
can call our power to account? – Yet who would have
thought the old man to have had so much blood in him.

LADY MACBETH, Macbeth, V, i

[155]

Tomorrow, and tomorrow, and tomorrow,
Creeps in this petty pace from day to day
To the last syllable of recorded time,
And all our yesterdays have lighted fools
The way to dusty death. Out, out, brief candle!
Life . . . is a tale
Told by an idiot, full of sound and fury,
Signifying nothing.

MACBETH, *Macbeth*, V, v

Lady Macbeth is dead; Macbeth will be soon.

Didst thou never hear
That things ill-got had ever bad success?

HENRY VI, *King Henry VI, Part 3*, II, ii

The purest treasure mortal times afford
Is spotless reputation.

THOMAS MOWBRAY, to Richard II, *King Richard II*, I, i

Though in the trade of war I have slain men,
Yet do I hold it very stuff o' the conscience
To do no contrived murder.

IAGO, *Othello*, I, ii

O, my offence is rank, it smells to heaven;
It hath the primal eldest curse upon't,
A brother's murder. Pray can I not,
Though inclination be as sharp as will:
... What if this cursed hand
Were thicker than itself with brother's blood,
Is there not rain enough in the sweet heavens
To wash it white as snow? ... But, O, what form of prayer
Can serve my turn? 'Forgive me my foul murder'?
That cannot be; since I am still possess'd
Of those effects for which I did the murder,
My crown, mine own ambition and my queen.
May one be pardon'd and retain the offence?
... O wretched state! O bosom black as death!

CLAUDIUS, Hamlet, III, iii

Tut! I have done a thousand dreadful things
As willingly as one would kill a fly.

AARON, *Titus Andronicus*, V, i

*Unlike Macbeth, Claudius, even Richard III, Aaron has no
conscience whatsoever; today he would be called a homicidal
psychopath.*

And oftentimes excusing of a fault
Doth make the fault the worse by the excuse.

PEMBROKE, to King John and Salisbury,
King John, IV, ii

O, 'tis too true!
How smart a lash that speech doth give my conscience!
The harlot's cheek, beautied with plastering art,
Is not more ugly to the thing that helps it
Than is my deed to my most painted word:
O heavy burthen!

CLAUDIUS, Hamlet, III, i

The speech he refers to is one of Polonius's sententious bits of advice to Ophelia, ending: 'that with devotion's visage/And pious action we do sugar o'er/The devil himself'.

This is the excellent foppery of the world, that, when we are sick in fortune, – often the surfeit of our own behaviour, – we make guilty of our disasters the sun, the moon, and the stars; as if we were villains by necessity, fools by heavenly compulsion, knaves, thieves, and treachers by spherical predominance, drunkards, liars, and adulterers by an enforced obedience of planetary influence.

EDMUND, King Lear, I, ii

Silence the conscience by blaming one's stars . . .

If to do were as easy as to know what were good to do, chapels had been churches, and poor men's cottages princes' palaces.

PORTIA, to Nerissa, The Merchant of Venice, I, ii

There is nothing either good or bad, but thinking makes it so.

HAMLET, to Rosencrantz and Guildenstern,
Hamlet, II, ii

To be, or not to be: that is the question:
Whether 'tis nobler in the mind to suffer
The slings and arrows of outrageous fortune,
Or to take arms against a sea of troubles,
And by opposing end them? To die: to sleep;
No more; and by a sleep to say we end
The heartache and the thousand natural shocks
That flesh is heir to, 'tis a consummation
Devoutly to be wish'd. To die, to sleep;
To sleep: perchance to dream: ay, there's the rub;
For in that sleep of death what dreams may come
When we have shuffled off this mortal coil,
Must give us pause: there's the respect
That makes calamity of so long life;
For who would bear the whips and scorns of time,
The oppressor's wrong, the proud man's contumely,
The pangs of despised love, the law's delay,
The insolence of office and the spurns
That patient merit of the unworthy takes,
When he himself might his quietus make
With a bare bodkin? who would fardels bear,
To grunt and sweat under a weary life,
But that the dread of something after death,
The undiscover'd country from whose bourn
No traveller returns, puzzles the will
And makes us rather bear those ills we have
Than fly to others that we know not of?

Thus conscience does make cowards of us all;
And thus the native hue of resolution
Is sicklied o'er with the pale cast of thought,
And enterprises of great pith and moment
With this regard their currents turn awry,
And lose the name of action.

HAMLET, *Hamlet*, III, i

In what is probably the most famous soliloquy in the theatre,
Hamlet contemplates the pros and cons of ending life.
His conscience – in this case, knowledge – balks at the
ungraspable prospect of being dead.

The Works
of William Shakespeare

It is almost impossible to date most of Shakespeare's works accurately. Plays were quite often acted as they were written – or, indeed, written as they were acted, as revisions became necessary or occurred to playwright and actors. The dates given here, of those works mentioned in this book, are approximations based on contemporary records and the educated guesswork of scholars of Shakespeare.

King Henry VI, Part 1 1589–90
King Henry VI, Part 2 1590–91
King Henry VI, Part 3 1591–2
Venus and Adonis 1592–3
King Richard III 1593
The Rape of Lucrece 1593–4
Sonnets (published 1609,
but in circulation in the 1590s)
The Two Gentlemen of Verona 1592–4
The Comedy of Errors 1592–4
The Taming of the Shrew 1593
Titus Andronicus 1593–4
Love's Labour's Lost 1594–5
King John 1594–6
King Richard II 1595
A Midsummer Night's Dream 1595
Romeo and Juliet 1595
The Merry Wives of Windsor 1596–9
The Merchant of Venice 1596–7
King Henry IV, Part 1 1596–7
King Henry IV, Part 2 1597–8

Much Ado About Nothing 1598–9
King Henry V 1599
Julius Caesar 1599
As You Like It 1599
Twelfth Night 1600–2
Hamlet 1601
Troilus and Cressida 1602
All's Well That Ends Well 1602–3
Measure for Measure 1603–4
Othello 1604
King Lear 1605
Macbeth 1606
Antony and Cleopatra 1606–7
Timon of Athens 1607–8
Pericles 1608
Coriolanus 1607–9
Cymbeline 1610–11
The Winter's Tale 1610–11
The Tempest 1611
King Henry VIII 1611–13
The Two Noble Kinsmen 1612–13
Cardenio 1612–13